SEASIDE GARDENING

SEASIDE GARDENING

By Theodore James, Jr.
Photographs by Harry Haralambou

Harry N. Abrams, Inc., Publishers

In loving memory of Laszlo and Mr. Fu

For Willy

Alas, the sea is calm

Page 1:
Lythrum salicaria 'Morden's Pink' and hydrangea

Title page:
In a garden in Northeast Harbor, Maine, blue pansies, white alyssum, astilbe, and hybrid Asiatic lilies are set against an old stone wall. The repeating patterns in the border create a somewhat formal effect. The flowers are iridescent in the vaporous late afternoon light.

Above:
Privet

Opposite above:
Daylilies

Opposite center:
Sedum and ferns

Opposite below:
Bayberry

Editor: Eric Himmel
Designer: Darilyn Lowe Carnes

Library of Congress Cataloging-in-Publication Data
James, Theodore.
    Seaside gardening / by Theodore James, Jr. ; photographs
by Harry Haralambou.
        p.   cm.
    Includes index.
    ISBN 0–8109–4451–0
    1. Seaside gardening.   2. Seaside gardening—Atlantic
Coast (U.S.)   I. Title.
SB460.J36   1994
635.9′5—dc20   94–32138

Published in 1995 by Harry N. Abrams, Incorporated,
New York
A Times Mirror Company

Printed and bound in Japan

CONTENTS

INTRODUCTION

*S*easide *Gardening* is intended, above all, to be as useful as it is beautiful, and so it limits its scope to the temperate regions of eastern North America from southern Canada south to North Carolina, an area with a climate similar to Northern Europe's and somewhat colder winters than the Pacific Northwest. Gardening is an art that is intensely influenced by nature, and no one book could possibly offer adequate guidance to coastal gardeners everywhere. The subtropical areas of Florida and Southern California can host plants that are too tender to be grown in the rest of the country (not for us are the palms of Palm Beach). On the other hand, they cannot support many of the hardy plants that the northern gardener relies on. Even the warmer temperate zones, such as the southern East Coast and the Pacific coast of Oregon and Washington, offer many species that would not survive farther north. Where climate is not a barrier, plants still may not travel far: an East Coast gardener could go a lifetime without setting eyes on the beach pine (*Pinus contorta*), a ubiquitous native of West Coast dunes and bogs from Mexico to Alaska.

To be able to show a range of seaside gardens, we chose to concentrate on two areas of the Northeast coast: the sandy beaches, wetlands, and rocky Long Island Sound shore of the east end of Long Island, and the rockbound coast of central Maine. For many generations, gardening has been taken very seriously in both of these areas (the first nursery on Long Island opened in 1737), and years of experience have left their mark on local gardeners. Long Island, with a seacoast and native flora that is in many ways typical of the lands that stretch north and south of it from Massachusetts to the Chesapeake, has always been and continues to be a focal point for innovative garden design, not only by gardeners, many of them artists, but by landscape designers and landscape architects who were employed by wealthy and sophisticated summer residents. Mt. Desert Island in Maine, where the coastal topography is quite different, has an equally splendid garden heritage, and for some of the same reasons.

The seashore offers a very special atmosphere. Under skies that seem bluer and clearer than those farther inland, hot colors are hotter and cool colors are cooler. A seaside garden shrouded in mist and fog offers an aura of mystery. Storm clouds may bring an ambience of surreal calm. Prevailing winds will toss its leaves like waves in the sea. The evening light is often spectacular, bathing plantings in a shimmering iridescence, while crisp clear mornings bring out the magnificent greens of nature. The invigorating salt air restores the spirit.

It is no wonder that so many residents of seaside areas turn to gardening as a primary pastime. Dropping the formality of city and suburban living, we get into our old garden clothes and relish the healthy exercise and rejuvenating, near spiritual, experience of gardening. There is nothing like a seaside garden to instruct us in the humbling wisdom that we are just one very small part of the entire scheme of God's earth.

In planning a garden, common sense is one guideline, and beyond that, experience, either one's

Native marsh mallows and reeds, both wetland plants,
flourish around a Long Island pond.

own or that of seasoned gardeners, is a great teacher. Most seaside gardeners have to contend with drought conditions during the hot days of summer: they are given sandy soil that drains quickly and prevailing winds that dry out plantings, and they soon learn that it is best to adapt and to bend to the will of nature by using plants that do not need constant watering. Along the rocky coast of Maine, gardeners utilize the small pockets of earth in rock crevices for plants that thrive in thin soil. On Long Island, traditional shade trees, most of which do not do well near the ocean, have been supplanted by smaller trees that do.

Sooner or later, seaside gardeners learn to take advantage of the sea's gifts. For example, they use silver foliaged plants to create contrast in foliage texture and color. Almost without exception, these plants originated in seashore areas and add stunning beauty to any planting. Their pale greens seem cool in the harsh, midday sun. Many gardeners go further and use flowers in cool colors—purples and blues with pinks. Others prefer summery, cheerful reds, yellows, and oranges. All have absorbed the hard lesson that a gardenesque look can be achieved by focusing on a few tried and true varieties.

Many seaside gardeners achieve stunning effects by including annuals in their plantings. These are generally pest and disease resistant, and more to the point, many are drought tolerant and thrive in the hot sun. And, since they live for only one year, it is not necessary to provide winter protection for them. Each year, growers, recognizing the demand for these plants, are offering more and more unusual varieties of seedlings. These days, gardeners are also encouraged to try native plants, which are naturally adapted to seaside conditions. Tough, graceful grasses, both natives and garden hybrids, are being used more and more in the place of traditional shrubs and herbaceous perennial plants to create structure in gardens.

My personal preference is for the "cool" garden. Except in spring plantings and in the early blooming rock garden, where vibrant color sparks the landscape, I rarely use orange, bright red, or sulfur yellow blooming plants in my garden, favoring the blue-purple-pink spectrum with white and pale yellow for accents. I also like plants with silver and blue toned foliage. This is the combination of colors that the English garden designer and writer Gertrude Jekyll used in her gardens. In this, I suppose, I declare my kinship to Maine gardeners rather than my fellow gardeners on Long Island, for the gardens of Maine surveyed in this book owe much to the American landscape designer Beatrix Farrand, who had a famous garden on Mt. Desert Island, and who was greatly influential in popularizing Jekyll's taste in colors in America. The reader, upon looking at the photographs of gardens designed by Tish Rehill, whose color sense is far more adventurous, may decide that I lack imagination, but I rarely have to worry about colors clashing in the garden and can concentrate on foliage, texture, autumn color, and other aspects of the plants. I love deep purple heliotrope with annual dusty miller or perennial lamb's ears. I am not charmed by hot red annual salvia, screaming yellow, orange, or gold marigolds, or the shocking electric blue annual lobelia. I am quite taken with old-fashioned single hollyhocks. The pale colors are favored around here, with a new one from Russia, a pale cream, given to me by an English friend two years ago. It will bloom this year and I am eager to see just what it will look like.

You will undoubtedly find, as I have, that your tastes in plants and color schemes will change with the years. I have all but phased out my temperamental modern roses, favoring the new English roses and the old garden varieties. Because heavy spring rain wreaks havoc with the stately tall blooming German irises and blowsy double pompon peonies, I now prefer shorter growing irises and have acquired many lovely single peonies. None of these need staking, and they are considerably less flamboyant. As the garden has grown and grown, I have found that I no longer have time to fuss with staking these plants. I am

The author's rock garden, Peconic, New York, designed with large sweeps of color. Already in late February, species crocus, Iris Danfordiae, I. reticulata, snowdrops, and winter aconite are all in bloom. This photograph shows the garden in May.

learning to make things easier for myself by growing plants that are more adapted to their natural environment.

In the pages that follow, you will find many beautiful photographs of exceptional gardens that we visited while gathering material for this book. You are bound to find ideas in them that you can adapt to your own property. Readers who do not have long experience gardening by the sea will find the chapter devoted to horticultural and practical advice especially useful. Finally, there is a plant list—what I call an "encyclopedic"— designed to help you to select plants for a seaside garden.

The Water's Edge

Two chairs on the lawn make a garden. In this case, the lawn consists of graceful native American beach grass, one of the few plants that will thrive in the sand directly on the ocean. It must be said that there are conservationists who would disapprove of any recreational use of the primary dune, that is, the first dune on the beach that protects low-lying inland areas from the fury of the sea.

An ambitious planting on a sandy bluff above the ocean on the east end of Long Island includes various perennials and annuals partly shielded from the wind by a hillock of rugosa roses, which also shelters a small pine. The garden, by designer Mary Beth Lee, includes dahlias, perennial phlox, chives, and, on the ocean side of the pool, a clump of zebra grass, and blends into the native flora of the dune. Looking toward the east, in a photograph taken at dawn (opposite above), we see sedum, fescue grass, Dahlberg daisies, and Swan River daisies. The perennial plantings are as permanent as nature permits this close to the ocean, while the annuals are added each spring.

This garden designed by Lisa Stamm and Dale Booher for a large house in Sagaponack, Long Island, is virtually surrounded by water. A stroll over the bridge takes one to the beach, while a few steps to the right, past a swimming pool, is a small estuary. The handsome planting comes as a surprise this close to the ocean, but none of the varieties is particularly difficult to grow: included are maiden grass (*Miscanthus sinensis* 'Gracillimus') and dwarf fountain grass (*Pennisetum alopecuroides* 'Hameln'), black-eyed Susan, Russian sage, purple loosestrife, sedum, and annual *Verbena* 'Sissinghurst'. The small trees that provide a extra measure of wind protection behind the border are Russian olives.

15

Artist Mabel d'Amico's Amagansett, New York, property looks out over the dunes to an inlet of Peconic Bay. A lovely planting of lavender, lilies, and candytuft protected by a hillock of ivy and Virginia creeper blends gracefully into the landscape, as do the clumps of daylilies beyond. Her studio window holds a sea of colored glass bottles, in colors that seem uncannily in tune with the plantings outside.

On the bank of a small estuary of Peconic Bay in Wainscott, New York, daffodils are welcome under the dreary skies of early spring. Among spring bulbs, daffodils are well suited to seaside environments, since they require little care, returning in profusion year after year, and are disease free. Rodents leave them quite alone as well, thank you.

The setting for the nostalgic garden opposite is a low, rocky promontory that juts out into Blue Hill Bay, Maine. Its old-fashioned charm suits the owner-designer, who, as a child, used to sail past the point and dreamed of one day building a house and living there. Well, now she does. Near the water's edge, the thin soil barely covers the rocks, and lichens, mosses, and a scattering of sedums carpet the ground. On higher ground, an old crab apple tree stands between the water and a flowerbed planted with white phlox, hybrid Asiatic lilies in a rainbow of colors, astilbe, salvia, and *Lythrum salicaria* 'Morden's Pink', all carefree perennials that adapt well to growing in soil pockets.

Surely Katie Dennis's garden overlooking Northeast Harbor is one of the area's most beautiful, with such old-fashioned favorites as hybrid Asiatic lilies, pastel-colored daylilies, *Liatris*, campanula, delphinium, and astilbe. Summers are rarely stifling in Maine, and so many plants that resent hot, dry climates, such as delphiniums, do very well here. Because of the late Maine spring, plants that are early bloomers farther south bloom in tandem with late spring and early summer perennials. The visual effect is stunning, as everything seems to be blooming at once. It is hard to resist a leisurely stroll down through Katie's garden to the water's edge.

On Mrs. Thomas Hall's property in Northeast Harbor on Mt. Desert Island in Maine, the woods come right down to the water. A path that meanders down to the rocks below is landscaped with dwarf evergreen shrubs, which are perfectly suited to conditions along the Maine coast.

Brian Beckman's house perches high above
the hustle and bustle of the fishing village
of West Point, Maine. On top of the rocky
ledge, where sturdy pines weather the off-
shore winds, he has planted a thriving vegetable garden in a mere one foot of added
top soil.

Seaside Landscapes

Close to the beaches on the barrier islands and in some areas of the coastal lowlands of the mid-Atlantic region, you will find yourself gardening in almost pure sand with a thin top layer of organic material. The Long Island garden (below), designed by Dean Peterson and George Lynch, is very close in spirit to a natural landscape and contains nothing but natives, with the exception of Japanese black pine. American beach grass, beach plum, and bayberry are all found in the wild up and down the Atlantic coast. Needless to say, the maintenance required by a garden like this is minimal, all of the plants are both adapted to and useful for binding very sandy soil, and despite the lack of a diversity of color and texture, the landscape has an inviting quality.

On low-lying lands near the sea, you may
encounter both freshwater bogs and salt
marshes. Freshwater bogs can occur surprisingly close to oceans and bays. This
mysterious, near primitive landscape at Fire
Island Pines, designed by Ken Ruzicka, was
a low-lying area subject to flooding during
periods of heavy rain. Since the water table
was a mere one foot beneath ground level,
he removed the soil and created a pond. It
is planted with edible wild watercress, *Nasturtium officinale*, which is native to the
area (this is usually available at pet stores in
the section devoted to tropical fish). Water
loving Japanese irises and yellow flag irises,
not in bloom at the time the photograph
was taken, are also in evidence, along with
many native plants.

At Carol Mercer's East Hampton garden, a large lawn leads down from the house to wetlands that edge a natural pond. Where the soil is very damp, she has planted moisture loving cultivars such as tall candelabra-form primroses (*Primula japonica* and *P. Vialii*), Japanese irises, and ferns. The pond is lined with pale pink wild roses, quite probably planted by birds. Where the ground is drier, astilbe, various grasses, and many other perennials that are averse to boggy conditions, thrive.

I can't recommend installing a lawn in large open areas close to the sea where the soil is sandy, unless you also install a staff of gardeners to care for it. Some creative alternatives are suggested by this series of photographs, which juxtapose late spring and mid-fall views of Carol and Alex Rosenberg's garden in Water Mill, New York, designed by Washington-based landscape architects Wolfgang Oehme and Jim van Sweden working closely with the owners. In the first two views (above), a meadow of catnip rolls up to a planting of various pampas grasses that offer cool green throughout spring and summer, and begin to sport their flamboyant plumage at the end of August. Two other views show a meadow planted with a sea of *Sedum spectabile* 'Autumn Joy' in spring and mid-autumn. A Japanese yew (*Podocarpus macrophyllus* var. Maki) seems to mimic the changing color of the sedum.

The mid-Atlantic coast boasts many sunny days throughout the summer. Why not take advantage of the sun to grow flowers? In this garden in Water Mill, New York, belonging to David and Lucille Berrill Paulsen, designer Elizabeth Lear created a grand wild-flower meadow. The oxeye daisies (*Chrysanthemum Leucanthemum*) and corn poppies (*Papaver Rhoeas*) are part of a seasonal progression of bloom that also includes blue bachelor's button, *Coreopsis lanceolata, C. tinctoria,* and black-eyed Susan.

In another Long Island meadow garden blessed with abundant sun, designer Elizabeth Lear planted a grove of Bradford pears to shade a charming gazebo. In the distance, *Coreopsis lanceolata* and C. *tinctoria* bloom amid fescue grasses and achillea.

Here, at a large Long Island seaside estate, Jane Lappin retained a group of native black cherry trees when she created the lawn that the client required. The graceful group echoes Matisse's masterpiece, *The Dance*. This is a good example of the way sea breezes lend character to tough trees by the phenomenon known as wind pruning.

The bluffs along Long Island Sound have a more moisture retentive soil and are more conducive to shady woodland plantings than the terrain on the South Shore. The grassy path at the Donald Currie–Daniel Gladstone garden in Southold (above), on the North Fork of Long Island, is edged by many plants suitable for shady conditions. Several varieties of hosta, including the stunning blue giant *H. Sieboldiana*, and blue flowering periwinkle make a cool but unobtrusive background for the planting. The tall *Viburnum dilatatum*, with its dazzling clusters of red berries which persist well into the winter, bears scented white blossoms in early summer.

The coast of northern New England is rocky and wooded, and fogs rolling in off the sea constantly water the ground. In a woodland area of Mrs. Thomas Hall's garden in Northeast Harbor, Maine, the characteristic outcroppings of ledge rock, rectilinear tree trunks, paths of shredded bark, and vast plantings of nurtured mosses evoke the tranquility of the moss garden at Saijo-ji in Kyoto, Japan. The tradition of Asian-style gardens on Mt. Desert Island goes back to the gardens designed by Beatrix Farrand for the Rockefellers in Seal Harbor in the 1920s.

Dorothy and Stephen Globus's garden, at Cornielle Estates on Fire Island, New York, on Great South Bay, is occasionally flooded with salt water during the winter. The combination of plants in this durable bed is quite harmonious, with silvery dusty miller, pale green *Sedum spectabile* 'Autumn Joy,' which is just beginning to show its pink summer color, variegated velvet grass, and Scotch broom. Trees include a corkscrew willow and a Russian olive. Brilliant orange marigolds, of a color difficult to use in most gardens, work quite well here, providing highlights for the scheme. Seaweed is gathered from the shoreline for mulch: not only is this practical, but it contributes to the very special seaside look of this pretty planting.

34

Designer Tish Rehill is known for her flamboyantly colorful plantings. This bed in a Southampton, New York, garden sets reds against yellows in a sea of green: purple foliaged sand cherry, which she has contained by severe pruning, purple leafed barberry, and startling scarlet *Crocosmia* 'Lucifer' for the reds; black-eyed Susans and *Coreopsis verticillata* 'Zagreb' for the yellows. *Gaillardia* X *grandiflora* 'Bremer' is diplomatic. The white flowered groundcover is *Mazus*.

Seaside Color

This beautiful garden, designed by Tish Rehill, shows the full effects one can achieve when working with the characteristic forms and colors of plants that are tolerant of the sandy soil of the mid-Atlantic seaboard. The plantings combine annuals in profusion (sunflower, cosmos, spider flower, dahlia, nicotiana, snapdragon), perennials (bugbane, astilbe, *Artemisia* X 'Powis Castle'), deciduous shrubs (*Spiraea* X *bumalda* 'Anthony Waterer'), and bulbs (hybrid Asiatic lilies). Notable are the use of grasses (including shimmering red-toned Japanese bloodgrass) where one would normally expect to find dwarf shrubs, and the absence of coniferous plants.

A lovely border in Sagaponack, New York, by designers Lisa Stamm and Dale Booher, frames a spectacular view of the wetlands beyond. The deep red grass is annual *Pennisetum* 'Burgundy Giant', often hard to find but well worth the effort. Pink dahlias, *Coreopsis* X 'Moonbeam', *Lythrum salicaria* 'Morden's pink,' yarrow, yellow daylilies, and a crop of blue irises complete the picture.

Jane Lappin's beds for a Long Island summer estate hark back with good humor to English antecedents (both cottage garden and landscaped park), what with the amusing sheep grazing on the grass in the foreground. This is a planting that starts out tall and gets only taller, rising to spires of hollyhock that seem to look down even on the masses of sunflowers. A wide variety of familiar perennials includes bugbane, astilbe, daylilies, *Coreopsis grandiflora* 'Sunray,' *Phlox* 'Blue Boy,' and *Lythrum salicaria* 'Morden's pink'

41

The pool house at another Long Island summer estate landscaped by Tish Rehill is almost covered with very vigorous Japanese knotweed (*Polygonum cuspidatum*), which is related to silverlace. In the adjoining border, she uses *Coreopsis* X 'Moonbeam,' old-fashioned Petunia 'Integrifolia,' and blue oat grass (*Helictotrichon sempervirens*) to produce a striking chromatic effect.

42

For this sweeping border leading up to the main house at a Southampton summer estate, Tish Rehill used hot colors—predominantly yellow, orange, and scarlet—that completely overwhelm cooler colors, for an effect that is almost jarring, particularly in the late afternoon, when this photograph was taken. She says that this palette is Mexican in inspiration, but it is remarkable how many yellow-flowered species thrive along the low-lying, sunny mid-Atlantic coast. Mrs. Thomas Hall's Maine woodland garden (pages 44–45), with not a yellow or orange flower in sight, makes an instructive comparison to this one. Among Rehill's favorite varieties are *Coreopsis* X 'Moonbeam', *Pennisetum* 'Burgundy Giant', Mexican sunflowers, and gaillardias (she favors G. X *grandiflora* 'Bremer,' 'Burgundy,' and 'Aurea Pura'). Notice how she has achieved a layered effect using plants of different heights from the front of the border to the back.

44

Mrs. Thomas Hall's extraordinary garden looks out over Northeast Harbor, Maine. The perennial plantings are set among trees and shrubs, chiefly coniferous evergreens that thrive in the moist climate of coastal Maine, away from the dessicating winds and sandy soils of the mid-Atlantic seashore. Shrubs are sculpted into mounds and drifts in the Japanese manner, but the perennial borders are English in inspiration and the palette limited to cool, largely pastel, colors, specifically pink, white, and blue. Among the favored varieties are astilbe (particularly A. *japonica* 'Rheinland'), annual white sweet alyssum, tall-growing meadowsweet (*Filipendula rubra* 'Venusta'), and Japanese and royal lilies. The blue end of the spectrum is held down by monkshood, an old-fashioned wild plant that has found its way into the most dignified and grand of gardens all over the world.

As you can see, the lush planting of delphinium, astilbe, phlox, lilies, and liatris in a Maine garden (opposite) is a stone's throw from the water's edge. A pocket of earth has been turned into a dazzling perennial garden.

46

Originally the Thuya garden at Asticou Terraces was a private estate on the slopes of Eliot Mountain in Northeast Harbor, Maine. Today it is a two-hundred-acre park and is open to the public. The gardens were originally created by Joseph Henry Curtis, a Boston landscape architect, who died in 1928. In 1988, landscape architect Patrick Chasse was commissioned to restore the gardens in keeping with the original design concept. The garden is a semi-formal herbaceous perennial garden in the style of English designer Gertrude Jekyll. Blue, white, pale yellow, and pink flowers are enhanced by the use of silver foliaged plants, a classic Jekyll combination. Many of the plants in the garden came from Beatrix Farrand's famous "Reef Point" gardens in Bar Harbor, Maine.

An elegant antique wrought-iron bench painted white is in perfect scale for this small flower garden in Blue Hill, Maine, filled with such old-fashioned perennials as phlox, astilbe, campanula, daylilies, monarda, and, in the back of the border, a clump of bugbane, with its white, feathery flowers. Here, on the verge of a meadow, the slightly unkempt lawn with its crop of dandelions has a rustic charm. Farther away from the water is a cutting garden (below) planted with some of the same varieties.

The magnificent cutting garden at Carol Mercer's house in East Hampton, Long Island, provides for flower arrangements throughout the house beginning in early June and well into the fall. A weathered picket fence lends character to the pretty scene.

Pools and Ponds

Pools and ponds seem to invite plantings that are primarily cool in palette. Barbara Slifka's pool in Sagaponack, Long Island (left), is landscaped (by designers Wolfgang Oehme and Jim van Sweden) with clumps of ornamental grasses and plants with primarily blue-green foliage; perhaps it is the garden itself that chills "The Frigid Bather." Flowering plants are carefully chosen to echo the cool colors and simple forms of the grasses: along the edge of the pool, two ball-shaped blossoms of *Allium giganteum* nod over masses of deep purple *Salvia X sylvestris* 'Mainacht.' Later in the season, globe thistle and catnip will carry on the cooling blue theme of the garden. In another Oehme–van Sweden garden (above), terra cotta pots planted with cerise lantana, a tender perennial that can be moved indoors during the winter, are placed next to beds of Russian sage.

People will differ about the esthetics of building modern swimming pools by natural bodies of water. One design strategy is to make the pool as unobtrusive as possible. The plantings surrounding this swimming pool, by landscape architects Dean Peterson and George Lynch, establish a smooth transition from a tailored but informal garden built principally around dwarf conifers and massed perennials to the wetlands in the distance. Incidentally, the outer ring of pines is a good example of a windbreak.

Architect Dale Booher's and designer Lisa Stamm's own pool at their Shelter Island, New York, house is flanked by a curtained Turkish folly. If you look carefully inside of the pool house, you'll notice that the interior is furnished with an upholstered banquette, far more comfortable to sit on after a swim than a wooden bench! Clumps of *Pennisetum* are installed here and there around the pool along with 'Betty Prior' roses, a single pink cluster-flowered variety that will grow virtually anywhere and flowers repeatedly through the summer, and hence is a good choice for seaside gardens.

58

People who choose to live or summer near the ocean often do so to be near water. Even the smallest property can have a lily pond, which·can be anything from the focal point of a baronial garden to, well, a tiny garden in itself. The lily pond above, designed by Ken Ruzicka for a garden in Fire Island Pines, is planted with irises, calla lilies, and English ivy. The trellis that serves as a backdrop is rendered in cedar; it screens a graceful stand of bamboo.

Lily ponds can be quite small (Lilypons Water Gardens sells a kit for a lily pond 28″ in diameter). This gently gurgling pool on the terrace of Mr. and Mrs. Stockton Andrews's house in Bar Harbor, Maine, is planted with water lilies and a clump of Japanese irises, arranged with some black stones picked up along the coast.

Bill and Erica Shank's white garden in Amagansett, is often called the Sissinghurst of Long Island by admirers. A formal reflecting pool is the focal point of a Romantic garden in the English style; it is planted with water lilies and banded bullrushes (*Schoenoplectus tabernaemontani* 'Zebrinus') and surrounded by a simple planting of irises and English ivy, accented by two urns planted with a yellow variegated variety of *Yucca filamentosa*. Several winters ago, when the Shanks had fish in the pool over the winter, raccoons played havoc around it.

These two lily ponds on Long Island summer estates on the ocean show different approaches to landscape gardening when cost is not a consideration. Both gardens are within the sound of the sea, but from Tish Rehill's extravagant planting for the lusher of the two (left), one would hardly guess that the ocean is a short walk away. Particularly notable is Rehill's use of colorful annuals to complement the perennial plantings, among them tricolor sage (*Salvia viridis*), goldenleaf sage (*S. officinalis* 'Aurea'), globe amaranth (*Gomphrena globosa*), and various yellow-foliage plants. Jane Lappin's pastoral landscape for a lawn by the ocean (above) focuses more attention on the trees and the pool.

White wicker furniture on a porch with a view of the sea makes for a nostalgic, old-fashioned ambience. No less traditional is a foundation planting of hydrangea. Above, pompon-shaped French hydrangeas and pink Meilland roses are underplanted with dusty miller. The larger shrub on the left is a lacecap hydrangea (*H. macrophylla*). Designers Lisa Stamm and Dale Booher have captured another era with their garden for this Long Island house situated on a beach behind the primary dune.

In open, sunny locations, grasses can take the place of traditional shrubbery. The linear architecture of this Long Island guest house is echoed by several large clumps of maiden grass placed with geometric precision on either side of the deck. White Adirondack chairs and two pairs of planters of geraniums complete the scene. It looks as though the house has sprung up in the middle of nowhere, which is exactly where it is.

The patio at Donald Currie and Daniel Gladstone's house on the Sound Bluffs in Southold, New York, is dominated by a shadblow tree. The garden works its way with pleasing informality around and among the square flagstones. Here is a good example of diverse foliage forms and colors used together to good effect, including hosta, dwarf conifers, sedum, and grasses. Except for the yearly installation of tender annuals, the plantings require little maintenance.

White wooden tubs planted with Hollywood juniper and pink hanging geraniums by designer Jane Lappin flank a doorway to a flagstone patio of a handsome house of white-rubbed brick. These junipers are very tough and can be left outdoors through the winter. As for privet, ivy, and hydrangeas, what is there to say? Gardeners on the East Coast have been combining them for over a century.

Here, as is often the case, the use of flagstones, along with wrought-iron furniture, gives the patio a more formal appearance. The ensemble, and the fountain in the brick wall that encloses it, are warmed by a perennial garden organized around four decorative urns with pink ivy-leafed geraniums spilling out of them.

67

The centerpiece of the elegant deck above, which was designed by Ken Ruzicka for a client in Fire Island Pines, is a beautifully pruned American holly planted in the ground beneath it. Other than the burgundy-leafed New Guinea impatiens in the large containers and the touch of geranium color on the roof of the guest house, the plantings are minimal, allowing the architecture, with its patterns of wood, to dominate the visual impact of the design. A purple-leafed flowering plum (*Prunus cerasifera* 'Thundercloud'), right, bears small pink blossoms in early spring and later little purple plums.

Growing through this deck by Ken Ruzicka is a thornless honey locust (*Gleditsia triacanthos* var. *inermis* 'Sunburst') with leaves that change from yellow in spring to bright green in summer. In July, highly fragrant white blossoms burst into bloom. The shade loving, pink-toned caladiums in the planter by the wall are an amusing match for the eccentric pink rocking chairs.

In many summer communities lot sizes frequently tend to be small and outdoor areas need to be screened for privacy. One common solution is the small deck with high walls, which can then be decorated with container plantings. These two examples, both by Ken Ruzicka for houses in Fire Island Pines, show formal arrangements and rely on those staples of seaside container planting: impatiens and geraniums. On one deck, below, the cascading Pronina junipers that look as if they are pouring out of their containers are quite extraordinary, as are the yellow-flowered marguerites (*Chrysanthemum frutescens*), which are trained as standards and, being tender, must be wintered indoors. The dwarf Alberta spruces together with the flamboyant mallows on the other deck, right, overturn one's expectation of the relative sizes of trees and flowers.

70

The word "deck" evokes a floor over water, which wouldn't be wrong in this case, since this structure, designed by Ken Ruzicka, overlooks a small freshwater pond. The pond was constructed of poured concrete, reinforced with chicken wire, and a colony of golden carp calls it home. The lush green planting of this tranquil spot includes cinnamon fern, English ivy, Piedmont azalea (*Rhododendron prinophyllum*), stonecrop (*Sedum spurium* 'Dragon's Blood'), creeping myrtle, candytuft, water lilies in the pond, and, for subtle touches of color here and there during the summer, white blooming hosta and pale day lilies.

More easily than a garden, a deck or patio can be turned into an exotic stage set for a summer. The owner of the house above has enhanced the tropical ambience of a white canvas cabana hung with gossamer swags of white mosquito netting with pots of red hibiscus, yellow gazanias, and even a pineapple.

Contemporary architecture frequently calls for simple geometric plantings that seem to lack playfulness and joy. Here Jane Lappin uses a series of tubs planted with collections of different annuals to create a sense of orderly profusion. Each one is planted with flowers of two primary colors and the spectrum in between. For example, the blue-purple-red planter contains *Brachychome*, *Nemophila*, red dianthus, dwarf gaillardia, and blue *Nolana*. In another there are yellow, orange, and red lantana, verbena, and *Pentas lanceolata*. *Helichrysum* 'Limelight', a cascading foliage plant of chartreuse hue, is used to set off the annuals.

An elaborate grouping of containers provides color on the deck of a house in Southampton, New York. Designer Mary Beth Lee has combined the hot pink of a scented geranium, cascading *Scaevola*, the purplish-blue blossoms of society garlic (*Tulbaghia violacea*), *Agapanthus africanus*, and white *Verbena canadensis*.

The light of the setting sun is caught in a planter at a house overlooking Shinnecock Bay in Southampton, New York. Designer Elizabeth Lear has created an outdoor "flower arrangement" in this tub. The swordlike foliage of dracaena gives structure to a planting that also includes ivy geraniums (*Pelargonium peltatum*), *Brachychome*, and variegated vinca. Lear recommends ivy geranium for seaside gardens because it is less susceptible to wind damage than other varieties.

Don't think for a moment that patio plantings must be modest. Take this romantic niche for a traditional English garden bench on a flagstone terrace by a pool in Long Island. To say that the border behind the fieldstone wall, by designers Lisa Stamm and Dale Booher, is planted with mostly undemanding perennials seems to miss the point. It includes *Geranium sanguineum* var. *prostratum*, *Nierembergia repens*, *Coreopsis verticillata* 'Moonbeam', *Lythrum salicaria* 'Morden's Pink', allium, white astilbe, and 'New Dawn' climbing roses trained on structures inspired by *tuteurs* designed by Monet for his garden at Giverny. The classical-style garden urns are planted with heliotrope, which will bloom later in the summer, petunias, variegated geraniums, and *Helichrysum* 'Limelight.'

78

Paths, Fences, and Trellises

What boardwalks are to the Mid-Atlantic coast, paths of pine needles and shredded bark are to the Maine coast. At the Thomas Hall garden in Northeast Harbor, one meanders up to an enchanting Japanese tea house that sits perched on the cliffs high above the water. This is truly a Maine forest look.

Boardwalks are a seashore institution. In Fire Island Pines, they are the only way to get around. The Pines retains many of the trees and shrubs native to the Mid-Atlantic barrier islands, including pitch pine, sour gum, highbush blueberry, and the two species that characterize the mature barrier island forest as it can be seen in the nearby Sunken Forest National Seashore: American holly and sassafras. To compose the landscape seen here, Ken Ruzicka added white birch, P.J.M. rhododendron, *Rhododendron prunifolium*, andromeda, a single red maple, cinnamon ferns, hosta, *Bergenia*, water lilies, and daylilies. Ground covers are used extensively, including English ivy, *Lamiastrum Galeobdolon* 'Variegatum,' snow-in-summer, and bugleweed. In the spring daffodils, clumps of lily of the valley and Virginia bluebells (*Mertensia virginica*) add color to the scheme.

Round House, in East Hampton, Long Island, was designed and formerly owned by Jack Lenore Larson. The bamboo that he planted at the entrance to the house almost ten years ago, opposite, has matured and now towers over the path, creating a cooling effect during the hot summer days, as well as the deep shade favored by the many shade loving perennials and ground-covers planted there today. The stark white stucco wall above, which separates the flower garden from the rest of the property, has a cooling effect in the deep shade. The laburnum tree, with its hanging yellow panicles, is traditionally paired with orna-mental varieties of allium, which are some-times difficult to grow. Chives, with their lavender blossoms, are an excellent and very practical substitute.

This elegant enclosed garden, designed by Lisa Stamm and Dale Booher, uses widely available annuals for color, in a palette that would have pleased Gertrude Jekyll herself: purple *Salvia farinacea* 'Victoria,' white nicotiana, and pink zinnias and cosmos. 'Heavenly Blue' morning glory climbs one of the tall trellises and box (*Buxus microphylla*) encloses the small parterres. Golden oregano (*Origanum vulgare* 'Aureum'), which is, of course, a culinary herb, edges the pathways.

The fence enclosing Mr. and Mrs. Stockton Andrews's Bar Harbor, Maine, garden, above, like the more refined fence, left, is a useful design for areas where deer are a problem, since it will discourage all but the most intrepid leapers but does not block out as much light as a solid fence. Many gardeners in summer communities add height to their fences by using bamboo poles instead of wood, which is heavier and more expensive. Here, the Japanese-style gate seems in keeping with the muted color tones of the planting, which includes pale lavender blooming hosta, white astilbe, and white Hybrid Asiatic lilies. Bolder colors are used only sparingly.

This enchanting gateway at Carol Mercer's East Hampton garden, is covered with *Clematis* 'Will Goodwin' and wisteria. Wisteria has its advocates and detractors and comes in and out of style. One advantage of using it by the water is that the salt spray and sand sap some of its legendary vigor, and it becomes a more well-behaved vine. The lovely "keyhole" effect of this gate arouses one's curiosity to see just what is beyond. Who could resist opening it and feeling that one is about to enter a very private place?

Designer Elizabeth Lear has used Nantucket ramblers ('Jeanne la Joie') with varieties of blue-flowering clematis over a moon gate in a Long Island garden. White double peonies bloom in front of a yew hedge.

English designer Charles Chesshire's clients in Amagansett longed for a "rose-covered cottage." He designed this planting on spanking white trellises. The roses that he selected include the climber 'New Dawn,' the hybrid musk rose 'Lavender Lassie,' which is actually rose-pink, and pink Meilland shrub roses. That's European dune grass under the stairs.

Another rose-covered cottage, this one in Water Mill, New York, was designed by Elizabeth Lear. To compliment the pink 'New Dawn' climbing rose, she has planted *Viburnum plicatum* 'Watanbe,' hydrangea, pink dahlias, and white snapdragons.

Katherine and Ralph Tise, of Corneille Estates, Fire Island, have decorated a shed with trellises and planters and installed an amusing bird house. Included in the planting are Montauk daisies, *Sedum spectabile* 'Autumn Joy,' dusty miller, purple loose-strife, and cosmos. The glossy leaved vine in the upper left of the photograph is catbrier.

The little cottage above with its window boxes of pale pink and white annuals, on the grounds of an estate in Northeast Harbor, Maine, is a favorite hideaway of children when they come to visit. The charming birdhouse is always full during the season. For whatever reason, birdhouses are rarely used by landscape designers, but people who create their own gardens almost always make room for one. There are always a lot of birds looking for food and lodging along the Atlantic coastline.

SEASIDE GARDENING: A PRACTICAL GUIDE

For the purpose of this chapter, I assume that you've never really gardened before. In this spirit, I am providing you with some information to help you predict what will or won't grow in your garden, given the conditions in your area, and some basic procedures about how to plant and maintain a garden by or near the sea.

I have two pieces of advice. First, gardening should be a satisfying and relaxing pursuit. Presumably, you are at the seashore to unwind, to spend time with your family and friends, to read, to swim, to do nothing, slowly. Don't overreach yourself. Second, remember that all good gardening practice involves a combination of experience and information. As soon as you begin to garden, you also begin to acquire both, and often too much of the latter, from fellow gardeners, books, catalogues, magazines, and newspapers. For example, clematis is a beautiful vine and easy to grow; pruning instructions for clematis are about as easy to follow as an IRS form. Don't despair. Plant what you like and have reason to think will thrive, and observe the results. This is the pathway to wisdom.

Assessing the Site

As a gardener, you want to know what plants will survive and thrive in your garden. To answer this question, you must be familiar with the general climate, weather, soil, and water conditions of your area. In general, climate is a constant, while weather, soil, and water conditions may change dramatically along a coastline.

The Agricultural Research Service of the U.S. Department of Agriculture has divided the United States into eleven plant hardiness zones for the convenience of gardeners and farmers. These zones are determined by average annual minimum temperature. Overall climate is the one area where seaside gardeners get a break over inland gardeners: because of the Gulf Stream, eastern coastal areas tend to be classified in higher zones than inland areas, and they experience the first killing frosts later in the fall as well. The Maine coast is considered to be in Zone 5 (–20° to –10°), the Massachusetts coast to Cape Cod in Zone 6 (–10° to 0°), and from Cape Cod south to the Chesapeake in Zone 7 (0° to 10°). You will frequently see these zones mentioned in garden catalogues and books and it's a good idea to plant varieties rated for your zone until you have a thorough knowledge of your garden's "microclimate": virtually every gardener knows someone who has a thriving specimen of a plant that allegedly can't be grown at that latitude. I have had great success in growing camellias, which usually have to winter under glass this far north, in my Eastern Long Island garden, with the oldest, a twelve-foot tall *Camellia japonica,* now in its seventeenth year.

Weather, soil, and water conditions along the Atlantic coast are much more difficult to predict. The sandy beaches and barrier islands that stretch from eastern Long Island south to the Carolinas offer very different opportunities to the gardener than Maine's rockbound coast, the Long Island bluffs overlooking Long Island Sound, or the coastline's numerous estuaries, tidewaters, and wetlands. One rule of thumb is that the closer you are to the ocean, the more steps you will have to take to provide a protected environment for a garden.

There are, in fact, numerous discrete environments or habitats along the Atlantic coast, but the gardener can make do with a few general guidelines. For the purposes of this book, I have adapted and simplified a classification system proposed by the Cornell Cooperative Extension Service of Suffolk County, New York, in a recent study of seashore plantings. Not surprisingly, given that the low-lying southern shores of eastern Long Island are so exposed to the ocean, this report emphasizes the importance of choosing plants that will "endure the harsh environment." As many of the gardens illustrated in this book demonstrate, you can, with careful design and horticulture, grow many more varieties of plants near the ocean than this advice suggests. Of the four "belts" listed here, the first three define areas directly on the water with differing soil conditions and exposure to wind and windborne salt spray. The fourth refers to immediate coastal areas not directly on the water.

Ocean Beaches

Gardens directly on ocean beaches are very vulnerable to damage by prevailing winds, windblown sand, salt spray, and occasional winter flooding, which few plants can tolerate year in and year out. Usually, unless they have been destroyed by development or storms, an ocean beach has a system of dunes that protect the land behind the beach. Naturalists call the dune closest to the sea the primary dune. Plants that are native to the primary dune—in the northeast, mainly American beach grass—act as dune stabilizers, slowing the wind at the surface of the dunes and helping to gather windborne sand. During storms, these root systems help hold sand in place, thereby slowing dune erosion. Any dunes behind the primary dune are called secondary dunes. The valley between the primary dune and the first secondary dune is called a swale. In practice, any property fronting an ocean beach is located in the swale (although in most cases, development has caused the leveling of secondary dunes to make way for more lots and storms may have leveled the primary dune), and the gardener directly on the ocean could do worse than work with what is growing in the swale naturally, such as beach grasses, bearberry, bayberry, beach plum, groundsel, red cedar, rugosa roses, and seaside goldenrod, and adding different plants judiciously.

Barrier Islands, Salt Marshes, Bays, and Estuaries

Barrier islands, peculiar to the east coast of North America from Georgia to New York, are narrow sandy islands that run parallel to the coast and are separated from it by shallow salt-water bays or lagoons. (Not all of the Atlantic islands are barrier islands. On bigger islands like Martha's Vineyard and Nantucket, for example, you will find a full range of seaside conditions.) On the barrier islands, there is far more exposure to breezes laden with salt spray than on the coastal plain because the land itself is virtually at sea level. The "soil," such as it is, is almost entirely pure sand (in Fire Island's Sunken Forest National Seashore, the sand is overlaid with a layer of organic material—made up of humus and decayed plant material—that is all of six inches deep). Here, and this holds true as well for low-lying bayfront land on the mainland, there is an amazing range of conditions that can affect the gardener. Dry lands adjoining salt marshes or bays can be difficult to plant because salt enters the groundwater from the bay. Only a few feet farther inland, the groundwater will be fresh. In general, shallow rooted plants will struggle to survive in sandy soil that does not retain water well.

Coastal Bluffs

Oceanfront properties atop sandy or rocky bluffs offer the gardener more options in terms of the variety of plants that will survive. The chief advantages conferred by elevation are that the soil will tend to be less sandy and there will be less exposure to salt spray during the growing season. For reasons having to do with the geological history of North America, you will find very little sand in the soil of Maine's coast.

Coastal Plains

The plain that stretches behind sand dunes or bluffs is naturally far more protected from wind, salt spray, and other natural forces, and usually offers less sandy soil as well. However, severe winter storms and hurricanes can carry salt water and gale-force winds many miles inland. The National Park Service estimates that in any one year, there is an 11 percent chance of a hurricane striking Long Island, and that a northeaster will cause "significant damage" somewhere along its coast almost every year. As you move north, the chance of catching a hurricane diminishes, while the strength of winter northeasters increases.

If you have a garden on or near the sea, refer to the encyclopedic at the end of this book for plants that will grow where you live. I have compiled these lists with an eye toward including a diversity of species that, for one reason or another, are likely to thrive in the environments described above. In general, plants that I have described as being drought resistant will probably adapt to the sandy soil of the barrier islands without special care and watering. The plants that will grow reliably on ocean dunes or

Snow fences are deployed on primary dunes to help prevent dune erosion, above, while clumps of rugosa roses, left, take root in the swale. Along a low, sandy bluff on the north shore of Long Island, below, Montauk daisies, yarrow, and seaside goldenrod help to bind the soil.

in bogs and wetlands are also noted. For further suggestions, consult with local nurseries and other gardeners.

Wind and Erosion

Your first step in planning a garden by the water is to afford your garden the protection it needs from the elements. Windbreaks not only serve to protect plantings, but they also make the outdoor areas of your property more comfortable. Don't make the mistake, however, of blocking the view that drew you to the house in the first place. Sometimes it's helpful to take snapshots of the property and then sketch in the plantings that you envision, to see how they will frame the view. Keep in mind that the area in the lee of the house, that is, the facade that faces away from the water or the prevailing winds, is protected by the house itself and may be the best site for a garden.

When installing a natural windbreak, use the toughest plants for the outermost wind-exposed area. Then, as you progress from the rim area, you can experiment with plants that are not so durable. See under shrubs and trees in the encyclopedic for recommendations of what to plant for windbreaks. Remember that even the most rugged species of trees will have difficulty establishing themselves in highly exposed situations and once established will exhibit growth patterns that are markedly different than what you will find inland. Japanese black pine (*Pinus Thunbergiana*), which is most often recommended for use as a shoreline windbreak (and which is now undergoing a blight along the East Coast), can grow up to 130 feet in optimal conditions, but would be hard put to attain 20 feet next to the ocean. In fact, a bulletin of the New York Cooperative Extension Service, recommends protection by a shoreline windbreak even for this species.

If your property is directly on the water and thus subject to the extremes of winter weather and storms, it is a good idea to provide some protection for newly planted trees, shrubs, and hedges in mid-fall. In short, your windbreak has to become established or else it will fall prey to the wind itself. To protect trees, first wrap the trunk with tree wrap. Then drive two stakes into the ground, one on either side of the trunk, leaning into the prevailing wind, and secure the tree to the stakes with old nylon stockings or rags (do not use rope, heavy-duty cord, or cable, as they will damage the trunk). Finally, and do this for newly planted shrubs as well, create a simple burlap cage to protect the branches. Drive wooden or metal stakes into the ground several feet from the trunk or main growth and then wrap burlap around the stakes to enclose the plant.

On oceanfront property, you must do what you can to build up the primary dune to protect your property from the erosion caused by storms and flooding, before thinking about windbreaks. In most coastal communities, the primary dune is subject to a complex web of laws and regulations. In New York State, for example, you cannot have sand moved from the beach to the dune without permits that are difficult to get. New Jersey, as of this writing, places heavy restrictions on what can be planted within 150 feet of beaches, bays, and rivers between Sandy Hook and Cape May. If the dune is barren of vegetation, common snow fencing can be installed to trap windborne sand and help build it up, as described by R. Marilyn Schmidt in *Gardening on the Eastern Seashore*. Place one fence at the base of the dune parallel with the shoreline and perpendicular to the prevailing winds, and another no further than thirty feet above the first. Alternatively, you can run fencing perpendicular to the prevailing winds at thirty foot intervals from a fence parallel to the shoreline. (More elaborate zig-zag patterns are also employed in some communities.) In the spaces between the fencing, you should, at the very least, plant our native American beach grass (*Ammophila breviligulata*), which spreads vigorously by underground roots. It is the fastest growing of the beach grasses appropriate for our climate. Plant small clumps about eight inches deep from mid-fall to early spring. Set at eighteen inch intervals in staggered fashion. Fertilize heavily with 10-10-10 fertilizer at the rate of 100 pounds per one-quarter acre in mid-spring and then again in mid-summer. Irrigate thoroughly to be sure that fertilizer gets to the roots of the plants. Some naturalists believe that a community of beach plants will hold the sand more effectively than beach grass alone, and that beach plum, groundsel, and seaside goldenrod, to name a few possibilities, should be planted with the beach grass.

Even if a garden is not directly on the water, some provision must be made to protect plants from wind. My garden is on the North Fork of Long Island, about one-quarter mile north of Peconic Bay and one-quarter mile south of Long Island Sound. The prevailing winds are from the west, and during the winter and well into the spring, they are nearly constant. I have screened this area with both a stockade fence and a dense hedge of Japanese holly, which provides substantial protection for my plantings, to the point that I have not found it necessary to mound my rose bushes, which are adjacent to the windbreak, during the winter. During the past twenty years or so, I have rarely lost a rose bush to the wind and cold of winter.

Salt Water

People living by oceans and bays whose gardens are frequently inundated with salt water, either from wind-blown salt spray or flooding associated with tides and storms, are naturally concerned about how the salt will affect their plantings. Curiously enough, inland regions of the American West, where soils in arid regions are naturally sandy and have high concentrations of salt, have provided the worst case scenario. Horticulturist Fred D. Widmoyer reports, in the Brooklyn Botanic Garden's bulletin on soils, that high salt concentrations can cause "inhibited seed germination, stunted growth, leaf scorch, wilting, and death of the plant."

Fortunately, under normal weather conditions, the salt spray carried by the wind does not cause severe problems for most plants in seaside gardens. However, plants that are constantly exposed to large amounts of wind-borne salt spray will become less efficient at absorbing water from their roots and may sustain injury. For this reason, if you have an open spot on your seaside property that regularly takes a beating from wind and waves, select and grow only the toughest and most salt-spray-resistant plants listed in the encylopedic.

Plants that are native to seaside environments have adapted in various ways to salt spray. For example, as you look through the list of recommended seaside plants, notice that many of them offer silver or gray foliage. If you look closely at the foliage of some of these plants, you will note that the silver color is created by a whitish fuzz, which protects the fleshy part of the leaf. Salt spray, which might otherwise damage the plant, is trapped in these minuscule hairs. Our native beach plums and bayberry, for another example, sport fruit that is waxy to the touch. The waxy surface protects the berries, which are essentially seed containers, from the salt spray. Some other native plants, such as sea grape, sea holly, and yucca, have glossy, smooth foliage that repel water. Still others, such as willow, Russian olive, and sea buckthorn, have very small leaves that shed water more efficiently than large leaves. All of these adaptations, not incidentally, account for qualities that can give seaside gardens their distinctive appearance.

In her book *Gardening on the Eastern Seashore*, R. Marilyn Schmidt points out that some plants actually benefit from salt spray, which seems to control fungal and insect infestations in roses, hollies, Austrian pine (*Pinus nigra*), lilacs, and zinnias.

Most plants are more susceptible to salt spray damage when the foliage is young, that is in spring or early summer. Mercifully, most severe seaside storms, such as gales, hurricanes, and northeasters, occur during late summer and well into fall, when the foliage has matured and toughened. During hurricanes and gales, salt water from the sea is swept up by the wind only to be released over the coast. Especially fierce storms may carry salt spray many miles inland.

Beyond thinking ahead, that is, selecting plants that resist salt spray damage, there are a number of things you can do to help plants recover from a heavy dousing of salt water. As soon as possible after a storm has passed, or even when it begins to wane, the most important thing to do is to hose down your plants, including trees, hedges, and tall shrubs, thoroughly and forcibly. Then flood the ground around the plants with fresh water. You want both to wash the plants and dilute the concentration of salt on the soil surface. Conifers and other evergreens usually sustain greater foliage damage than deciduous trees, since the plants do not drop their foliage in the fall.

If the salt spray has been especially severe, deciduous trees may lose their foliage. This happened on the east end of Long Island and in Connecticut during September of 1987 when the severe winds of Hurricane Gloria came from the south, bearing much salt spray from the Atlantic Ocean, Long Island Sound, and Peconic Bay. Shortly after the storm passed, the leaves on the trees turned an ugly brown and fell to the ground. However, much to everyone's amazement, the trees sported new buds, which then leafed out, creating a second spring. Many spring-blooming shrubs—forsythia, rhododendron, azalea, kerria, and lilac—also bloomed again that fall. The following spring, all was back to normal, and the plants displayed their usual glorious, colorful, blossoms. After Hurricane Gloria struck, some of my neighbors did indeed hose down everything to remove salt spray, but many who did not lost little, if anything, from their gardens. Waterfront properties did suffer greater losses, although the long term consequences of the storm, except where plants were uprooted or broken by the high winds, were not nearly as devastating as we expected.

During severe storms, low-lying land at the seashore is often flooded with salt water. This rarely causes permanent damage to plants unless poor drainage causes the salt water to stand on the soil. Most gardens will weather freak salt water floods, and you can help them by irrigating them as soon as the flood water subsides with generous amounts of fresh water to wash the salt out of the soil, assuming that your drainage is good.

More serious is persistent salt water flooding or the presence of salt in the groundwater. In planning seaside plantings, be aware of low-lying areas, try to ascertain whether or not they flood frequently, and plant salt-tolerant species if you are in doubt. Often, the presence of the groundsel tree (*Baccharis halimifolia*), a native of coastal marshes that can tolerate high concentrations of salt around its roots, is a sign that there is salt in the groundwater, usually from a nearby bay. Areas that flood regularly and retain standing water should be dealt with thoughtfully. Before you try to drain or fill in a bog or salt marsh, it is best to consult a professional landscape architect or engineer for advice. Remember, also, that there may be laws that forbid filling in or altering the wetland and estuary areas of the seaside environment.

Soil and Sand

Sand is not soil. Of the sixteen elements known to be essential to the growth of most plants, thirteen— that is, all but carbon, hydrogen, and oxygen (and some of the nitrogen)—originate in the parent rock from which soil develops. The white sand beaches characteristic of the Atlantic coast south of Maine are 98 percent weathered particles of quartz, a medium that is unusually poor in the minerals that most

The view toward the wetlands adjoining Carol and Alex Rosenberg's house in Water Mill, New York, above, is a meadow of reeds, Phragmites australis, a Middle Eastern native that may be the most broadly naturalized plant in the world. While it would be unwise to plant reeds (many naturalists lament that they are everywhere crowding out native species), it is often the better part of wisdom to leave them undisturbed in wetland areas unless you are really adept at gardening with natives.

plants need. The closer you are to the seashore, the more sandy your soil is likely to be, and the poorer in elements essential for plant growth.

Furthermore, without constant watering during the summer, plants that are not drought resistant tend to dry out quickly in sandy soil, suffering severe stress. Prevailing winds cause them to transpire moisture rapidly through their leaves, but they are growing in a medium that does not retain moisture effectively around their roots. To improve the moisture retentiveness of sandy soil and to provide necessary nutrients, it must be enriched with organic matter: humus, compost, peat moss, decayed leaves, or top soil. Many seaside gardeners grow rapturous about the value of seaweed—the eelgrass (*Zostera marina*) that washes up in vast quantities along bay shores along the Atlantic coast and is free for the taking—as a mulch and soil-builder. It is indeed an excellent mulch, and does not need to be washed with fresh water as many gardeners seem to believe, but its one drawback as a soil-builder is that it contains very little nitrogen and decomposes slowly. If you want to try to improve your soil with seaweed alone, also add an extra source of nitrogen like fish meal. The more organic matter you add to sandy soil, the greater the variety of plants you will be able to grow. As a rule, you should excavate areas you plan to plant to a depth of one foot, then mix the excavated soil with about one-half to two-thirds as much organic material (see "Planting and Maintaining Hardy Plants," below).

Most gardeners learn about their soil and what can and can't grow in it by experience and observation. For example, when you browse through catalogues or books, you will occasionally see it mentioned that a certain plant is known to prefer acidic soil or alkaline soil. The relative acidity of a soil is measured by its pH value, and can be ascertained by testing, but it's not something you should worry about unless you have reason to think that there is a problem with your soil. (In general, soils in the eastern United States tend to be acidic, but sandy seashore soil is often alkaline.) If you're worried about soil problems, you can have your soil tested by your local County Extension Service, which you can find by looking in the telephone directory under "County Offices." (In Maine, apply directly to the Soil Testing Laboratory, Department of Plant and Soil Sciences, University of Maine, Orono, Maine 04469.) There is usually no charge for this service, and they will not only test the soil but provide recommendations about how to go about improving it and suggestions of what to grow.

If your soil is very sandy, and you can't afford to improve it on a large scale, you can create pockets of improved soil throughout your property. Another alternative is to build raised beds on top of the soil, making containers for good soil using treated lumber, bricks, stone, or even concrete. If you need to clear a space for a garden and you want to embark on a long term soil improvement program, consider recycling the brush, twigs, and leaves that you remove from your property rather than having them carted away. You can hire a local garden service to come to your property to clear, chip, and shred this material, and you will be surprised to see how it breaks down into soil over time. Finally, do not overreach yourself: remember, beautiful and distinctive gardens have been created using only varieties that are completely adapted to seaside conditions, planted in sandy soil enriched with seaweed.

Special Care for a Seaside Garden

If you want to grow any plants other than native species in the sandy soil of the Atlantic coastline south of Maine, there are certain steps you should take to ensure that they are protected against loss of precious moisture and receive the nutrients that they need.

Beyond adding organic matter to sandy soil to improve moisture and nutrient retention, there is another way to conserve moisture: mulch! The soil around all plants should be covered with at least two to three inches of organic mulch. Not only will this protective layer serve to conserve moisture and reduce the concentration of surface salt, by slowing water evaporation from the soil, but it will also cut down on weed growth and, as the organic material breaks down, it will add nutrients to the soil.

There are many different materials that you can use for mulch, and your choice will depend in part on what is available and what you think looks good. The best is homemade compost (which is simply decomposed plant residues, usually mixed with manure). With a little bit of effort and planning, you can have large supplies of what gardeners call "brown gold" at a very good price . . . for nothing. Even if you don't purchase or build a composter, you can simply make a compost pile in an inconspicuous corner of your garden by alternating six-inch layers of organic plant material, including wet vegetable garbage from the kitchen such as coffee grounds and vegetable parings, along with leaves, grass clippings, seaweed, and weeds, mixed with some soil, and two-inch layers of manure. The pile should be roughly flat or concave on top, to conserve as much moisture as possible. Experience shows that you need about a cubic yard of material to generate compost. After a season or so, you will have plenty of compost to enrich the soil and to use as mulch.

Oak leaves and pine needles provide an airy cover for the ground and improve the soil. Other leaves, such as maple leaves, tend to mat on the surface of the soil and can be harmful to plants unless they are reduced to compost. A two-inch layer of beach stones can be quite attractive around trees, hedges, or shrubs that are growing within the brickwork of a patio. They will help to conserve moisture and keep the weeds down, although they do not add nutrients to the soil. Eelgrass also makes an excellent mulch.

If you opt to purchase mulch from a nursery, garden center, or landscaping service, it's probably best to use salt hay or wood chips, usually cedar or pine, in the smallest size you can find. Although the large chips may look reasonably attractive, they do not decompose readily enough. If you use wood chips, you should be aware that they will monopolize the nitrogen available to your plants while they decompose, and fertilize accordingly. Buckwheat hulls are too light to use in windy seaside environments, as are cocoa shells, which can be somewhat distracting in a garden on account of their chocolate scent. I cannot recommend grass clippings or peat moss.

Fall plantings should be protected by a six-inch layer of mulch to protect them over the winter. While hardy plants will not be harmed by the cold, constant freezing and thawing of the surrounding soil can cause them to heave up out of the ground. The salt hay keeps the soil at a more constant temperature, making it less likely that a plant will heave.

Well-mulched soil retains moisture well, but during prolonged periods of summer drought, you will still need to water to a depth of a foot to a foot-and-a-half at least once a week. You can check this by digging a place in the garden where plants do not grow, but which has been watered. Lay down drip hoses, available at garden and home improvement centers, in your garden and leave them there for the growing season. These are preferable to conventional sprinklers, which lose water to evaporation and run-off. If local ordinances prohibit watering, you really need to plan your garden using only the most drought-tolerant species.

Finally, you should fertilize your plantings, particularly if you are gardening with non-native species. For best results, work about one tablespoon per square foot of all-purpose 5-10-5 fertilizer into the soil around each plant each spring before growth commences. If your soil is decidedly sandy, you should fertilize more frequently, because inorganic nutrients leach out of sandy soil very rapidly. Be careful not to overfertilize plants (more often than not, fertilizer runs off into the ground water, where it can do more harm than good).

Trees and Shrubs

You are now the proud owner of a small property on or near the ocean. Chances are good that you are using it as a summer house. If you are really lucky, you'll be able to spend the entire summer in this paradise. More likely, you'll use it on weekends and perhaps for several weeks in July or August. If you want to have a garden, the first question to ask yourself is how much you need to change in the way of major plantings, and how much that is already there you can live with.

First, find out what you already have. Ask the help of a knowledgeable person or buy a field guide that covers your area, and try to identify the trees and shrubs that are already growing on your property. Unless you have a really clear idea of what you want to do, leave the existing trees and shrubs alone for a season and see what they're like.

Often, there's a reason why they're there in the first place. If you were wondering why Ken Ruzicka (see page 81) would design a garden around such native trees as pitch pine, sour gum, American holly, and sassafras, ask yourself (as he surely did) what other trees would have a chance of becoming established on a low-lying, boggy stretch of barrier island. Remember also that many trees grow no faster than you do. If, like Katie Dennis (see page 19), you have a hillside of handsome shade trees and conifers rolling down to the water, consider that it would be a generation before anyone in your family has such magnificent shade again, should you cut them down.

I'm not saying, never fell a tree or yank out a shrub and plant a new one. Just think about it first. That said, there are many uses for trees and shrubs. They can be used as single specimens to provide focal points in the garden, in foundation plantings, as windbreaks, as plantings to control erosion, to provide shade, in shrub borders or hedges along the sides, back, or front of your property for privacy, and in borders to divide one area of your property from another. For windbreaks, people generally rely on a few tough coniferous species. Privacy barriers are also usually composed of evergreens. Deciduous trees are customarily used to provide shade or as ornamental specimens. Imaginative gardeners have made hedges out of many curious plants, but traditional hedging species are dense shrubs that take pruning well. If you mix deciduous shrubs, dwarf conifers, and broad-leaved evergreens, you can have a carefree planting that offers interest throughout the season.

You can buy hardy plants (trees, shrubs, grasses, herbs, and perennials), either at a nursery or garden center, or from a mail-order company. Whatever you do, I recommend that you write away for catalogues from some of the mail-order companies listed in the back of this book: your fantasies will be much more exciting if you do. If you buy your plants by mail, it's best to get your orders in by January or February to be sure that the plants you want will not be sold out, but you can continue to place orders through the end of May. Most mail-order nurseries will ship your plants at the appropriate planting time for your region. Will trees and shrubs be healthier or "fresher" if you buy them at a nursery? Not necessarily: very few nurseries and garden centers grow their own stock; most purchase it from wholesale dealers, and even though you may buy the stock locally, it does not necessarily mean that it was grown locally. A tree or shrub purchased "on the ground," so to speak, may not be better, but it is likely to be bigger, than anything that comes in the mail, which may be decisive for you if you're in a hurry to see your garden as you envision it. Just don't expect the breadth of selection locally that you see in catalogues. Finally, if there's a local gardening service that has a good reputation, you might use it for purchasing and planting trees. A good service will take responsibility for the long-term health of the tree, and replace it if something goes wrong.

Trees and shrubs are usually sold in containers or bagged and burlapped (called B & B in the garden business). The burlap is usually very loosely woven and will eventually rot, so it is not necessary to remove it before installing a plant. For seaside environments that are particularly harsh, container grown plants stand a better chance of surviving than B & B stock. Avoid bare root stock, and be careful of B & B stock late in the season, for if the nursery hasn't been conscientious about watering, what you take home may resemble a cannonball with a stick in it rather than a tree. Perennial plants other than shrubs and trees are almost always sold in containers.

General instructions for planting and caring for trees and shrubs are given below.

Perennials

If shrubs, hedges, and trees are the backbone of the landscape, certainly perennial flowering plants are the backbone of a seaside flower garden. They are long-lasting and winter hardy, that is, each fall their stalks wither and die, only to grow again from the roots, or crown, the following spring. (You will see them referred to as "herbaceous" plants, which means that, unlike shrubs and trees, they have almost no woody tissue that survives from season to season.) While you do not have to plant them each spring as you do annuals, they tend to bloom for a shorter span of time than annuals, some in late spring, some in summer, and some in fall. For this reason it is wise to plan carefully when planting perennials.

Perennials can be used in many different ways in a garden. Ambitious gardeners group them together in flowerbeds called borders (if they form strips between a walk or lawn and a wall) or island beds (if they are open on all sides). This can be a complicated art, whose aim is to achieve a harmonious blend of colors and forms that changes throughout the spring and summer. Perennials can also be used to brighten the landscape after spring-blooming bulbs have finished, to add color to monotonous foundation plantings, to brighten driveways and paths, and to accent garden structures. The perennial cultivars that I have included in the encyclopedic adapt well to a seaside garden, are generally readily available, and are, to a great extent, pest and disease free. Technically, some of the varieties that I have listed under "grasses" and "herbs" in the encyclopedic are perennials, since they are hardy and bear new flowers every year, and as you can see from the photographs in this book, grasses and herbs are important plants in seaside garden borders and beds, as, indeed, are annuals. (See pages 38–39 for a good example of a border that mixes perennials, grasses, and annuals.)

One of the most satisfying ways to expand your garden is by taking extra perennial stock from friends, family, and neighbors, since most experienced gardeners know that to maintain vigor, most herbaceous plants must be divided regularly and replanted. Don't be shy about asking, for every garden begins this way. One word of warning! Be sure to have the donor identify her offerings. Avoid just sticking any old plant you have been given in the ground, willy-nilly, without knowing exactly what it is. If you do, the result will most likely turn out to be an unruly hodgepodge of heights, textures, and blossoms, often in clashing colors. If someone does give you unidentified stock, you can always plant it temporarily in what gardeners call a holding garden, that is, a place where they can watch a plant grow to maturity for a season or two and then decide exactly where it will or will not work in their garden.

Digging wild plants for your garden is not a good idea. It is much better to identify the plant you like and purchase new stock or seeds from a native plant nursery. For years, Long Island gardeners have dug up beautiful specimens of butterfly weed from roadsides, almost always with unfortunate results for the plants (and the natural landscape). Meanwhile, this plant is easy to grow from seed, and widely available from nurseries.

Planting and Maintaining Hardy Plants

Although spring is usually the time when gardeners install new plantings of shrubs, hedges, trees, and perennial plants, recent research has shown that early fall is also a good time. A plant's roots continue to grow until the very cold days of January or February—long after the rest has gone dormant—and a strong root system is what a plant needs to endure the dry heat of summer. Seashore areas, where seasonal temperatures are sustained almost a month longer than inland, are ideal for fall planting, always remembering that any plants in very exposed situations should be planted in the spring so that they have the summer to acclimate themselves. On low-lying land by the water and barrier islands, you should probably forgo the pleasure of fall planting. By the way, it is especially necessary to mulch fall plantings to guard against winter heaving.

Before you start digging a hole for a particular plant, be it a tree, shrub, or other perennial plant, take a quick eye measurement of the root ball in the container or in the burlap binding. The rule of thumb for planting is to dig a ten-dollar hole for a five-dollar plant, that is, under normal conditions, make the hole twice as wide and twice as deep as the root ball. In a seaside environment, particularly if you are dealing with a soil that is primarily sand, perhaps a hole three times as wide and twice as deep is best. (Digging in sand is easy.) Assuming that you haven't improved the soil on your entire property, now is the time to mix about two-thirds organic material (topsoil, compost, peat moss, eelgrass, or well-rotted manure) with one-third of the excavated sandy soil. Even if your soil is already excellent, it is still a good idea to enrich the area where you intend to plant with organic matter. Fill the hole with the enriched soil and water it thoroughly; it's a good idea to let it settle for a day before planting in it.

Planting is a cinch. Remove the soil you prepared the day before, position the plant in the hole at the level at which it was grown at the nursery, and fill in beneath, around, and on top of the roots (or root ball), tamping the soil and watering as you work, to ensure that you are not leaving any air spaces around the roots. When you are done, water the plant thoroughly and tamp the soil firmly. Water once more. Be sure to leave a slight depression in the soil around the plant to facilitate watering throughout the season.

Give your plants growing space. Don't cramp shrubs and trees. In perennial plantings, a good rule of thumb is that tall-growing plants should be planted two feet apart, medium-height plants eighteen inches apart, low-growing plants twelve inches apart, with tiny, miniature plants perhaps six inches apart.

Most plants need very little care beyond the general watering and feeding instructions given above. The one chore you should get in the habit of doing is to deadhead your perennials, that is, remove the spent blossoms. Not only does this make the plants look better, but in some cultivars, it helps to produce a second bloom. You don't deadhead flowering trees and shrubs (thank goodness), but you should remove old flower heads from lilacs, azaleas, and rhododendrons to improve next season's blooms. Unruly shrubs and vines can be pruned in the spring, with the exception of certain plants that bloom only from old wood and should be pruned right after flowering—experience and the specific horticultural instructions that come with each plant are good teachers in this regard. Always prune damaged trunks and branches in the aftermath of a storm.

Remember, no plant is immortal. When a perennial becomes overgrown or seems to have lost its vigor, dig up the plant in the spring, divide it (that is, break the crown gently into several pieces, each with its own roots), and replant what you want to keep. Give the rest to an aspiring gardener down the street.

Bulbs

Among the greatest pleasures of spring for the gardener are hardy, spring-blooming bulbs—both the "major" varieties: daffodils, tulips, hyacinths, and crocuses, and the often overlooked "minor" varieties: scilla, grape hyacinth, snowdrop, and the charming glory-of-the-snow—as well as irises, lily of the valley, and allium. Of course, if you do not live in or visit your seaside home during the spring, you may decide not to install any spring-blooming plants. That is a decision you will have to make yourself. There are also summer-blooming bulbs, particularly lilies, to enjoy.

You can plant colorful beds or borders using only bulbs, include bulbs in mixed beds with perennials and annuals, or scatter them on the ground and then just plant them where they have landed, for a natural effect. Many bulbs will become naturalized, that is, multiply and spread from year to year without human intervention. Planting requirements for bulbs are modest. Most want either full sun or partial shade in order to perform well. The exceptions are allium, which prefers only full sun, and lily of the valley, which prefers partial shade. Very few thrive in deep shade, so avoid areas under evergreen trees, foundation plantings with northern exposure, and other areas of little sunlight. Bulbs will rot in waterlogged soil and require good drainage to grow properly, so if there is any area on your property that is subject to regular tidal flooding or to salt water flooding during severe storms, avoid planting bulbs there. That said, I can report that friends of mine who live on Peconic Bay had severe flooding from Hurricane Bob and their daffodils survived the ordeal unscathed, blooming quite profusely the following spring. Bulbs are virtually insect and disease free, and a bit of soil preparation at fall planting time and some annual feeding is about all the maintenance that they require. And every year, beginning in late winter, they reward you with dazzling and glorious displays.

All spring-blooming bulbs must be planted in the fall. Minor bulbs should be in the ground by the end of September, daffodils by the end of October, and tulips can be planted as long as the ground is workable. Summer-blooming bulbs, most of which are tender and must be dug in the fall and stored over the winter indoors, should be planted in the spring, after all danger of frost, with the exception of lilies, which are hardy and can be planted in either spring or fall. Toward the end of summer, spring bulbs start to appear on the shelves of nurseries, garden centers, and even supermarkets. There are also mail-order nurseries that offer huge selections. It is a good idea to write for catalogues by June and to place your orders by the end of July or early August. Most mail-order nurseries deliver bulbs at the proper planting time for your area.

When you go to the garden to plant bulbs, be sure to bring a ruler with you so that you can gauge planting depth and spacing properly. As a rule, plant bulbs about three times as deep as their diameter. You will also need fertilizer. For many years it was universally thought that bone meal was an essential fertilizer for bulbs; experience and research have indicated that although it will not hurt the bulbs, neither does it help them. All-purpose 5-10-5 fertilizer appears to provide whatever nutrients bulbs need. Dig a hole twice as deep as the recommended depth for the bulbs you are planting and mix fertilizer with soil at the rate of one tablespoon per square foot, three-quarters of a cup per ten square feet, or four cups per fifty square feet. Replace the soil to the recommended planting level and flatten out the bottom of planting hole by patting it gently with your hand to provide an even surface for the bulbs so they won't fall on their sides in the hole when you fill it in with soil. Set the bulbs in place with the pointed ends up and press them gently into the soil. Cover them, tamp the soil down lightly, and water thoroughly. If there are dry spells in your area during the fall, be sure to water the planting at least once a week. Spring bulbs can be given a dusting of 5-10-5 fertilizer at the rate of one tablespoon per square foot when they begin to emerge from the ground. Plantings of summer bulbs will benefit from a six-inch mulch to conserve moisture, to keep weeds down, and ultimately to fortify the seaside soil.

After bulbs bloom, you can remove spent blossoms but not the leaves, which supply the bulb with nutrients for next year's bloom. Allow foliage to wither and dry naturally, then you can remove it. If you find the withering leaves unsightly, tie them up in bundles with string or rubber bands or hide them by overplanting the area with annuals.

Annuals

I am a great believer in using annuals in the garden. Annuals are plants that live for a season, growing from seed in the spring, bearing flowers that go to seed, and dying with the first frosts, completing their life cycle in this short span of time. Almost all annuals bloom throughout the summer and early fall, and some continue past the first frost. A handful start blooming in late spring, particularly if they are given a head start.

Annuals are indispensable to the seaside gardener, who must believe that every year can be a fresh start. How many gardeners in recent years have returned in the spring to their summer houses on the shore, only to find that winter storms and flooding have buried their perennial beds under drifts of sand and stunted vines that were once engines of growth? What a pleasure to contemplate the possibility of planters full of impatiens or a wall covered with morning glories. Even the summer renter can create a private paradise of annuals.

There are two ways you can have annuals for your seaside garden. You can purchase flats of seedlings, which are often called sets, at garden centers and nurseries. This is the sure-fire way to secure almost instant color in your garden. It is also a way to grow certain annuals that, because they require a longer growing period in order to flower in time for late spring and summer, must be started indoors under lights long before the appropriate outdoor planting time. You can even purchase full-grown plants. The disadvantage of this approach to growing annuals is that the industry still offers little more than about a dozen cultivars in a dozen or so varieties of each as seedlings, and these are the most common annuals grown. When you restrict yourself to these offerings alone, you have merely scratched the surface of the many charming plants available to you.

The other way to grow annuals is to purchase seeds and grow them yourself. Whether you purchase your seeds from supermarkets, garden centers, nurseries, or mail-order houses, you can choose from among many more varieties. However, and here's the hitch, some annuals require a much longer time than others to germinate and grow to flowering stage. Furthermore, some seeds should be sprinkled on the soil surface and kept evenly moist at all times because they require light to germinate, while others should be planted and covered with soil, because they require dark conditions to germinate. So, if you wish to sow seeds directly into the ground, you must limit yourself to those varieties that can be planted outdoors early in the spring, those that will grow to flowering stage quickly, and, unless you have the time and inclination to provide evenly moist conditions for surface sown seeds, those that should be covered with soil when planted. Even with these restrictions, there are many varieties that you can grow successfully by sowing their seeds directly in the soil either in early spring or after frost. Some of these are listed in the encyclopedic.

Fortunately, it's a simple matter to avail yourself of varieties that do need a head start indoors. With a small investment of time and money, you can make a simple fluorescent light structure to start seeds (a small manufactured unit will cost you about four times as much), and new worlds of plant adventures will open up to you.

Here's how you do it. Purchase a four-foot long industrial fluorescent light fixture. They cost between ten and twenty dollars in most home improvement centers. These fixtures usually come with two cool tubes. Substitute one warm tube for one of the cool tubes. There is no need to buy expensive, plant growing fluorescent tubes. Despite manufacturer's claims, results for starting seedlings are equally good with one cool and one warm tube. Either hang the fixture in a heated basement over a table or work bench or attach it to the bottom of a shelf in the house. You are ready to start seeds indoors at the proper time.

As the fixture should remain on for about fourteen hours a day, you may want to buy a timer if you don't wish to be bothered with the daily task of turning it on and off. You can start with one fixture, but you will soon find that you need at least two. Eventually, you will want three or four to accommodate all the plants you wish to start from seed. (As I write this, I have eleven in my basement!)

You can sow seeds in just about any container imaginable: milk cartons, plastic containers, flower pots, aluminum trays, in short anything that will hold a seed-starting soil mixture. Drainage must be provided, so if you use homemade containers, poke holes through the bottoms so that excess water can escape. There are also many products available in garden centers and nurseries that are made specifically for starting seeds. I use APS (for Accelerated Propagation System) seed-starting kits, available from Gardener's Supply Company in Burlington, Vermont. These are made of styrofoam and include a reservoir arrangement that maintains even moisture for the seed trays for about a week between watering. The APS-40 has forty compartments for planting seeds and is fine for most annuals. The APS-25 has twenty-five larger compartments and is more useful for starting vegetables from seed. A clear plastic top makes the unit a mini-greenhouse, assuring faster germination of seeds (don't forget to remove it after the seeds sprout). A four-foot industrial fluorescent light fixture will accommodate three of these self watering seed starter trays.

You will also need the proper soil to start plants indoors. Do not purchase potting soil, as it is too heavy in texture to start seeds. Use a seed-starting medium like Terralite or Reddi-Mix, and moisten it thoroughly before planting the seeds according to the instructions on the packet, that is, either lightly covered with soil or on the soil surface. Start several seeds in each individual compartment, if you are using seed trays. Label the containers carefully and place them under the lights with the soil surface about two inches from the light tubes. Raise the lights as the plants get bigger. If you are using homemade containers, mist with room temperature water using a mister available in garden centers and nurseries to keep the soil evenly moist.

When seedlings are about one-half inch high, cut off all but the strongest in each compartment. Feed once a week with all-purpose liquid house plant fertilizer at one-quarter the strength recommended by the manufacturer. Most annuals can be safely planted outdoors "after all danger of frost": a good rule of thumb is to follow the recommended time for planting tomatoes outdoors in your area. About one week before planting them outdoors, you must "harden off" your annuals. This is to acclimate them to strong sunlight and cool nights.

For the first couple of days, place the containers outdoors in a shady spot during the day and bring them inside at night. The third day, put them in the sun for about half a day and in the shade for the other half. Finally, leave them in the sun for the entire day and bring them indoors only if the night is to be chilly. In any event, if it rains bring them indoors. If the plants start to look bleached, they are receiving too much sun and are not yet accustomed to the strong light. Move them back into the shade. After about one week, you can safely plant them in your garden where you want them.

Taking care of annuals is a cinch. Most prefer full sun and are not fussy about soil. Plant and mulch as you would perennials, keeping in mind that annuals that are quite small at planting time can become rather large very quickly. Annual plantings are, to a great extent, maintenance free. The one thing you must do is to deadhead spent blooms, that is, cut faded flowers before they go to seed. The reason you do this is not just esthetic but to extend the their period of bloom. Once seeds have formed, the plant has accomplished its purpose, that is to regenerate itself, and it will stop flowering. By deadheading, you frustrate this process and keep the plant blooming until frost.

Containers

You can grow virtually anything in containers, including plants that won't normally thrive in typical seaside conditions, *as long as they are watered regularly*. Many tropical and subtropical plants, which are not hardy in northern climates, can be grown outdoors in containers in the summer and then brought indoors to a greenhouse or a sunny area in the house for winter enjoyment. Just remember that a small pot in full sun in hot weather may need watering once a day. If you can't be around to water every day, try filling a large container with peat moss, wet it thoroughly, then place a smaller container planted with annuals in the middle. You can mask the edge of the smaller container with more peat moss.

The range of containers you can buy is vast, but beyond this selection, imaginative gardeners use just about anything that will hold soil to grow plants. The only essential thing is to be sure to provide drainage holes and a one-inch layer of pebbles or flowerpot shards in the bottom of the container for drainage. Beyond that, a simple soil mixture that is highly retentive of moisture is called for, either one-third garden loam, one-third compost, and one-third peat moss or one part garden loam to one part vermiculite or perlite. Before planting, thoroughly soak the planting medium. Most gardeners plant their containers in the spring after all danger of frost is past. While they are occasionally used for herbs, scented geraniums, and perennials, containers are usually planted with annuals.

Pests

Many insects, reptiles, birds, and animals are the gardener's friends. Ladybugs, wasps, praying mantises, and fireflies consume not only the eggs of many harmful insects, but in some cases kill the insects themselves. Birds offer colorful plumage and lovely songs, and some eat their weight in insects every week. Bats also are great insect eaters, consuming thousands of mosquitoes a day. Bees pollinate flowers and make honey. Butterflies add much beauty to the garden. Toads consume ticks and many other harmful insects; snakes eat rodents, such as moles and voles. If you have an outdoor pet cat, he too will help to keep moles and voles under control.

However, not everything in nature loves a garden. If your plants do not look healthy, inspect them carefully to determine what may be the problem. It is a good idea to bring a magnifying glass to the garden with you to expedite diagnosis. You can purchase remedies for the most common insect and fungal infestations. If you opt for chemical treatments, which are available at most nurseries and garden centers, always follow the manufacturer's instructions when using them, to protect your health and the environment. In many seaside communities, the water table is high and chemicals are rapidly passed to it through the upper soil layer, so you should take special care when using pesticides and fungicides.

If you decide you do not want to use chemical sprays, use botanical sprays. Two that are effective are Rotenone and Pyrethrum. Beyond that, many insects can be controlled with a spray made up of a half-and-half solution of dish washing detergent and water. However, don't expect a single application to rid your plants of pests. You will have to persist and spray every day for a week or so, and even then results are not guaranteed.

Small Animals

Rabbits and other small mammals are particularly hungry during the early days of spring, when plants that make up their normal diet may not have leafed out. They seek what they can, just to survive. Now we all have some compassion for their hunger, but not when they level the emerging buds of our autumn dreams, that is the bulb plantings that we worked so hard at planting last fall. Be thankful for small favors: they don't like daffodil, narcissus, crown imperial, snowdrop, *Iris reticulata, I. Danfordiae*, lily of the valley, and scilla. They are ravenously addicted to crocuses and tulips. How many times have gardening friends told you that rabbits absolutely leveled every one of their emerging crocuses and/or tulips to the ground? I know gardeners who have totally given up on planting tulips and crocuses for this very reason.

However, take heart, for there are humane solutions. Dried blood, available in garden centers by the bag, works for me. Beyond repelling our friends with the big ears, it is excellent fertilizer for bulb plantings. As soon as you see the tiny, green shoots of crocuses or tulips emerging from the ground, and this can be as early as late January, sprinkle some dried blood on the planting. Then, after each rain, and you must be meticulous about this, repeat the application. I've done this for the past ten years or so and now have established plantings of crocus and even tulips that have perennialized. I have also found that laying small pieces of chicken wire over a planting until the buds open works. Rabbits just don't seem to want to walk on wire mesh, and I can't say that I blame them. I remove the mesh when the crocuses bloom and when the tulips reach about eight inches in height, carefully slipping it over the blossoms. If you notice that new growth on some of your perennials is being eaten, try the dried blood and chicken wire treatment until the foliage and emerging buds are about a foot high.

Unfortunately, dealing with moles and voles is not as easy. If you find yourself walking on grass that seems to sink beneath your feet, if there are long ridges of crumbled soil on the lawn, you probably have an infestation of moles on your property. Moles tunnel beneath the ground in search of insect grubs, which usually congregate around the roots of grass, plants, or bulbs. The moles eat the grubs, but leave the plants alone. The only way you can get rid of the moles is to get rid of the grubs, which involves spreading all kinds of poisonous insecticides on the soil surface.

"Well, if the moles don't eat the bulbs, why should I worry?" you ask. Sometimes nature plays funny tricks. At work here is an insidious conspiracy, for after the moles make the holes in quest of the grubs, the voles, which resemble tailless little moles, go into the holes the moles make and tunnel through to the roots of plants and bulbs. Like the rabbits, they do leave certain bulbs quite alone, thank you very much, but most are three-star fare as far as they are concerned.

Before I learned how to frustrate them, I had installed about one thousand bulbs, major and minor, in a rock garden here. The sandy soil in the garden, nicely warmed up by the rocks, was child's play to the moles and the voles. All of the bulbs bloomed the first spring, and then through the summer and fall the voles cleaned out the entire planting. The next spring all that came up were the snowdrops, daffodils, and scilla. A friend of mine, who had installed an extravagant bed of tulips, was strolling through his garden with friends and admiring the planting. Suddenly, right before their eyes, one of the tulips disappeared into a hole in the ground.

I had read somewhere that if you lined planting holes for tulips, crocus, and other favored bulbs with mesh gutter wire, it would frustrate these creatures. I tried it and it did help somewhat, but by the second year, most of my bulb plantings were cleaned out. Then, several years ago, I was in northern

The Charles Simon garden in Seaview on Fire Island was especially designed with the collaboration of the late Jimmy Viles to welcome deer, and the owner puts out trays of food to attract the beautiful animals. It is essentially a bamboo grove with the addition of some conifers.

Portugal at the garden of vintner Antonio Guedes and I noticed the mole-made ridges in his lawn. I asked Guedes if he had mole and vole problems and he told me that he did, but that he had come up with a solution. Wherever he wanted a planting of tulips, he excavated the area, then sunk heavy-duty plastic or rubber pots into the soil, with the rim of the top at soil level. These pots all have drainage holes, necessary for any plant container, as professional growers use them to ship and sell perennials, shrubs, and trees. Then he would fill them with soil and plant as usual. I tried it in my rock garden and it worked. I have several plantings of species tulips which are now in their fifth year, apparently vole proof.

Voles not only attack spring-blooming bulbs, but fruit trees, some perennials, shrubs, and ornamental trees. There isn't really much you can do about them: if a healthy plant suddenly seems to expire, chances are the voles are eating the roots.

In some seaside environments, notably those along the rocky coast of Maine, or the Connecticut and Long Island shores of Long Island Sound, chipmunks chew away at many varieties of plants. Like moles and voles and rabbits, they savor crocuses and tulips. They also eat many varieties of annuals and perennials. Mrs. Thomas Hall, of Northeast Harbor, Maine, has come up with a kind solution to preserve the plantings in her stunning Japanese garden. She sets "Havahart" traps for the chipmunks. Once they're caught, she picks up the traps and drives several miles from her house and releases them. Although she still has some chipmunk damage, the trapping and transporting help somewhat.

Deer

Now we are talking big game. On Fire Island, off the coast of Long Island, deer are ubiquitous and wander through the various resort communities unafraid of human beings. They are very tame, will approach you for a handout, and have learned how to open garden gates that are not securely latched. Once inside a garden, they eat almost everything in sight. In other areas of seaside Long Island, where they are not quite so contained, they have also become quite blasé about human beings, sitting around and sunning themselves like odalisques on waterfront decks. The story is the same up and down the East Coast: deer populations have risen dramatically in residential areas over the past twenty years.

Although studies have been made to determine just what plants deer like or dislike, none are conclusive and all are riddled with practical contradictions. There are some plants that appear to be reasonably deer proof, but, when their preferred food is in short supply and they are in danger of starvation, deer, like any living creature, will eat just about anything that grows in order to survive (as the Dutch ate tulip bulbs during the German occupation of Holland).

Beyond installing tall fences (see pages 84–85)—they must be at least seven feet high to keep deer out—or electric fences, there are some steps you can take to protect your plants. All newly installed trees and shrubs should be wrapped with tree wrap or Tubex, available at garden centers and nurseries and from many mail-order companies. Deer are particularly hungry at the end of winter and in early spring, when there are few foliage plants around to sustain them. If you do have favorite plants that you wish to protect, provide some sort of cage fencing for them.

Deer repellents like Ropel, Chew-Not, Deer Away, Bobex, and Hinder are available at garden centers and nurseries. Sometimes these work if you follow the package directions very carefully and start application before the damage is done. You need to repeat applications often, particularly after rain or snow may have washed the deterrents from the plants.

More to the point, it makes sense to select plants that deer do not usually like to eat, although even this often does not work, for deer will develop a taste for a particular plant if they have had to eat it during famine periods.

Unfortunately, the intense debate about the widespread presence of deer in residential areas up and down the East Coast is finally not about nibbled plantings. To understand why so many gardeners are so troubled by the white-tailed deer, one need only turn to the publications of the Suffolk County, Long Island, Department of Health Services on Lyme disease, which are all decorated with bold drawings of stags.

Ticks and Lyme Disease

Despite the fact that the mere mention of ticks is enough to depress most gardeners, you must protect yourself against a tick-bite inflicted case of Lyme Disease (first identified as an illness in Old Lyme,

Deer and Plantings

Karen Jescavage-Bernard, in her book *Gardening in Deer Country*, indicates that the following plants are to be avoided if deer are a problem in your area: andromeda, azalea, fir, holly, lupine, mountain laurel, spruce, X *Cupressocyparis leylandii,* yew, and all fruit trees. To confuse matters further, a recent trial in Seaview on Fire Island demonstrated that even during the early growing season, deer did not eat andromeda. Other plants that they seemed to avoid were bluebeard, box, and lamb's ear.

In the summer of 1993, the Cornell University Cooperative Extension Service in Westchester County, New York, asked master gardeners in that area to keep records of plants that were rarely eaten by deer and of plants that deer seemed to favor. People who live in areas with large deer populations and comparatively little native foliage, that is, on the shore, may find this study to be overly optimistic. These are some of the results that were obtained.

Plants rarely or never eaten by deer:

ANNUALS: Ageratum, cleome, dahlia, dusty miller, forget-me-not, foxglove, gaillardia, geranium, heliotrope, lobelia, marigold, morning glory, parsley, poppy, salvia, snapdragon, sweet alyssum, sweet basil, thistle, verbena, and wax begonia.

PERENNIALS AND BULBS: Allium, amsonia, artemisia, astilbe, baby's breath, balloon flower, baptisia, bergenia, bleeding heart, buddleia, butterfly weed, campanula, candytuft, chives, cimicifuga, cinnamon fern, columbine, coreopsis, crown imperial, daffodil, dianthus, echinops, eupatorium, evening primrose, feverfew, flax, garlic, goldenrod, heath, heather, lamb's ear, lavender, lily of the valley, loosestrife, monarda, oregano, oriental poppy, ostrich fern, painted daisy, partridgeberry, plumbago, purple coneflower, ribbon grass, rosemary, royal fern, sage, sea lavender, Shasta daisy, spurge, tiger lily, veronica, yarrow, and yucca.

GROUNDCOVERS: Ajuga, aurinia, lamium, pachysandra, and vinca.

VINES: Bittersweet, clematis, honeysuckle, and wisteria.

Plants occasionally eaten by deer

ANNUALS: Pansy and sunflower.

PERENNIALS: Geranium, English ivy, iris, rudbeckia, and sedum.

Plants often eaten by deer

ANNUALS: Hollyhock, impatiens, and Mexican sunflower.

PERENNIALS AND BULBS: Crocus, daylily, hosta, phlox, rose, and tulip.

Connecticut, in 1975) and know how to treat it if you are gardening along the East Coast. It is caused by a bacterium (a spirochete) and is transmitted primarily by the deer tick. If there are deer or field mice in your area, there will be ticks, for these animals carry the ticks from place to place on their bodies. Incidents of the disease have been reported in almost every state, but it is most prevalent in eastern coastal areas from Maine to Massachusetts.

Lyme disease is sometimes difficult to diagnose. Deer ticks are very small—the nymph is about the size of a poppy seed—and people rarely notice them on their bodies until after they have been bitten. The most characteristic early sign of Lyme disease is the appearance of a rash at the site of the tick bite that slowly expands during the ensuing weeks. It may become as large as fifteen inches in diameter, but it will vary from person to person and not all people who get Lyme disease will develop the rash. Even if untreated, the rash will eventually fade. Other early symptoms of the disease are fever, headache, neck stiffness, muscle and joint pains, enlarged lymph glands, conjunctivitis, or even general fatigue.

It is unwise to leave the disease untreated. The most common late complication of untreated Lyme disease—coming weeks to months after the initial infection—is swelling and pain in the large joints, especially the knees. In 15 to 25 percent of untreated patients, neurological complications may eventually occur, and fewer than 7 percent of untreated patients develop irregular heartbeats or other cardiac problems.

If you are are bitten by a tick or if you think you might have Lyme disease, you should consult a doctor, and preferably one who is familiar with the disease. Prompt treatment with antibiotics is usually effective.

There is no way that an active gardener can completely protect himself against tick bites in seaside areas that have deer and rodent populations. Deer ticks rest on vegetation wherever deer are found, and are brushed onto humans or animals as they pass by. The spring, when the ticks are in the nymph stage, and therefore most difficult to detect because of their small size, is precisely when most gardeners are busiest and usually not in the mood to take cumbersome precautions. However, certain measures should become habitual: you should wear light-colored clothing with long pants and sleeves, tucked into socks and gloves, when you garden in areas with underbrush; you should check yourself and your companion or children once a day for ticks; you should check your pets regularly for ticks; you may want to use tick repellents containing the chemical DEET on your clothing (following the instructions carefully).

You can also try to manage your property so that the potential deer tick population is reduced. Deer ticks are found in heavily shaded, damp areas with abundant leaf litter and undergrowth, where their host animals also congregate. Fence deer out; mulch borders and shrubbery carefully; remove leaf litter from areas where you will be gardening or relaxing; and admire the brush-covered areas of your property from afar and try to keep kids and pets out of them.

There are pesticides that can be used to curb the tick population, but most of us are uncomfortable with the idea of exposing ourselves and our loved ones, not to mention our neighbors, to the possible long-term effects of pesticides. One habitat-targeted product is Damminix, which is disseminated in cotton balls that are supposed to be attractive to mice as nesting material, and is the equivalent of dusting field mice with tick powder. According to the Cornell Cooperative Extension Service, the impact of Damminix on tick populations in New York State trials has been disappointing. If you use it, follow the instructions carefully.

We can only hope that science will eventually discover a vaccine that will protect us all from the bite of these dreadful creatures.

PLANT ENCYCLOPEDIC

The following list includes plants that can be recommended for seashore planting on the East Coast of North America. Species that are especially suited to the seashore environment, particularly those with a high tolerance of drought, are singled out with a ♣. Within this group, plants that can survive directly on dunes are also noted.

Experienced gardeners will, no doubt, be able to point to many plants that are missing from this list, and it is not intended to be exhaustive or exclusive. Rhododendrons and azaleas, for example, are among the easiest of flowering shrubs to grow if you have a bit of light shade and a moisture retentive soil; they are shallow rooted, however, and do not generally do well in dry, sandy soil, bright sun, and dessicating winds, and so they have been omitted. This should not be taken to mean that you cannot, with a bit of care, grow a rhododendron near the sea.

A word about native plants. The word "native" in this list is used generally to describe plants that are native to the East Coast, and it is given because it is useful to know which plants are naturally adapted to the conditions in which you are gardening.

Annuals

All of the following annuals can be grown in all climates until a light or killing frost, depending on variety.

Ageratum
Clusters of soft, powder puff blossoms in various blue shades, as well as white and pink. Medium-green foliage. 12–24″ depending on variety. Thrives in partial shade, in ordinary soil. Needs some moisture. Start indoors under lights eight weeks before last frost date in your area. Surface sow. Do not cover seeds as light is needed for germination. Plant seedlings outdoors after all danger of frost. Deadhead throughout season for continuous bloom. Ageratum combines well with pale yellow-blooming and silver-foliaged plants.

Antirrhinum (Snapdragon)
Spikes of single, double, and butterfly-shaped blossoms in all colors except true blue. Medium-green foliage. 6–48″, depending on variety. Thrives in full sun, in enriched soil, but will tolerate some shade. Needs some moisture. Start indoors under lights eight weeks before last frost date in your area. Surface sow. Do not cover seeds as light is needed for germination. Plant seedlings outdoors after all danger of frost. Pinch tips of plants when about 3″ tall to encourage branching. Then pinch again when new shoots are 3″ tall. For continuous bloom, deadhead spent flower stalks. Snapdragons often winter over in moderate climates. Usually the second year's bloom is even more spectacular than the first. Because taller varieties must be staked, select from dwarf or medium height varieties.

♣ Arctotis (African daisy)
Brilliant yellow, salmon, apricot, orange, or white daisylike flowers. Gray, woolly foliage. 12″. Thrives in full sun and well-drained soil. Drought resistant. Seedlings resist early spring cold. Sow seed in situ as early in spring as ground is workable. Cover seeds with soil or planting medium according to package directions. For continuous bloom, deadhead spent flower stalks.

Begonia Semperflorens-Cultorum Hybrids (Wax begonia)
Pink, salmon, coral, red, or white, and bicolor clusters of blossoms. Stiff, waxy deep-green or bronze-toned, rounded foliage. 3–12″, depending on variety. Thrives in partial shade and enriched soil, but tolerates full sun. Needs some moisture. Start indoors under lights six weeks before last frost date in your area. Surface sow and gently press seeds into moist, planting medium. Do not cover seeds as light is needed for germination. Plant seedlings outdoors after all danger of frost. It is not necessary to deadhead spent flowers for continuous bloom.

♣ Brachycome iberidifolia (Swan River daisies)
Soft blue daisylike flowers. 12″. Thrives in full sun and ordinary, sandy soil. Resists drought. Start

indoors under lights eight weeks before last frost date in your area. Deadhead for continuous bloom.

Calendula officinalis (Pot marigold)
Yellow, gold, orange, apricot, or cream single and double daisylike blossoms. Medium-green foliage. 24″. Thrives in full sun and in ordinary soil. Needs some moisture. Seedlings resist early spring cold. Sow seed in situ about four weeks before it is time to set out tomatoes in your area. Cover seeds with soil or planting medium according to package directions. For continuous bloom, deadhead throughout season. Flowers are edible and can be used as a garnish in salads.

Calliopsis, see Coreopsis

Callistephus chinensis (China aster)
Red, pink, purple, blue, or white pomponlike blossoms. Dark-green foliage. 6–30″, depending on variety. Thrives in full sun and enriched soil, but partial shade extends life of individual blooms. Needs some moisture. Start indoors under lights six weeks before last frost date in your area. Cover seeds with soil or planting medium according to package directions. Plant seedlings outdoors after all danger of frost. For continuous bloom, deadhead spent flower stalks. This is one of the most popular of all annuals, especially for fall gardens. Avoid planting asters in the same place two years in a row, as they will not thrive in the same spot the second year.

♣ Celosia cristata (Cockscomb)
Brilliant red, orange, apricot, yellow, and fuchsia blossoms. Medium-green foliage. 9–24″. Thrives in full sun and well-drained, enriched soil. Drought resistant. Sow in situ, after all danger of frost. Thin to about 12″ apart. Deadhead regularly to encourage more bloom. Blossoms of varieties in the Plumosa group are feathery. Many gardeners consider Celosia garish, and the colors can be overwhelming in a garden.

♣ Centaurea (Cornflower, bachelor's button)
Blue, pink, white, and maroon thistlelike flowers. Silver-green foliage. 24–30″. Thrives in full sun, in ordinary soil. Drought resistant. Seedlings resist early spring cold. Sow seed in situ about four weeks before it is time to set out tomatoes in your area and cover seeds with soil or planting medium according to package directions. For continuous bloom, dead-

head spent flower stalks. Cornflower is easy to grow, but if you fail to deadhead after bloom plant will bloom itself to death and become unsightly by midsummer.

Cineraria maritima, see Senecio Cineraria.

♣ Cleome (Spider flower)
Large rose, pink, lilac, purple, or white spiderlike blossoms. Lobed foliage. 3–6′. Thrives in full sun and light, sandy loam. Drought resistant. Seedlings resist early spring cold. Sow seed in the place you wish them to grow about four weeks before it is time to set out tomatoes in your area. Surface sow. Do not cover seeds with soil or planting medium since light is needed for germination. For continuous bloom, deadhead spent flower stalks. Although stems grow tall, they are quite sturdy and rarely need staking. Easy to grow. Cleome self-seeds freely once established. Local lore where deer are plentiful holds that they will not eat Cleome.

Coleus
Grown for colorful foliage in brilliant red, mahogany, green, yellow, white, blue, or rose. To 24″. Thrives in partial shade in enriched soil. Needs some moisture. Surface sow outdoors after all danger of frost. Do not cover seeds with soil or planting medium since light is needed for germination. Keep constantly moist until established. Exotic foliage adds a tropical touch to any garden.

Consolida ambigua (Rocket larkspur, annual delphinium)
Blue, red, white, pink, or purple spikes of florets. Medium-green foliage. 3–4′ Thrives in full sun and enriched soil. Needs some moisture. Seedlings resist early spring cold. Sow seed in situ as early in spring as ground is workable, or sow in fall, as seeds will winter over nicely but will not germinate in warm weather. Cover seeds with soil or planting medium according to package directions. For continuous bloom, deadhead spent flower stalks. A good substitute for delphiniums, which can be difficult to grow. Self-seeds freely in most areas.

♣ Coreopsis basalis/Coreopsis tinctoria
Yellow, orange, red, maroon, or crimson daisylike blossoms. Medium-green foliage, depending on variety. 8–48″. Thrives in full sun, in well-drained soil. Drought resistant. Seedlings resist early spring cold.

Sow seed in situ four weeks before it is time to set out tomatoes in your area. Sow where plants are to bloom as *Coreopsis* resents being transplanted. Where winters are mild (Zones 7–9), sow seed in fall. Cover seeds with soil or planting medium according to package directions. For continuous bloom, deadhead spent flower stalks.

♣ *Cosmos*
Bright clear red, rose, pink, yellow, white, or crimson daisy-shaped blossoms. Feathery foliage. 3–6′. Thrives in full sun, in ordinary, well-drained soil. Drought resistant. Sow in situ outdoors, after all danger of frost. Cover seeds with soil or planting medium according to package directions. To encourage branching and thus more flowers pinch tips of plants when they are 12″ high and then again when 18″ high. For continuous bloom, deadhead spent flower stalks. Cosmos self-seeds freely once established and attracts birds.

♣ *Dianthus* (Pinks, carnations)
Brilliant-colored scarlet, salmon, white, yellow, pink, or crimson carnation-shaped blossoms on attractive silver-green foliage. 6–36″. Thrives in full sun, in ordinary, well-drained soil. Drought resistant. Sow in situ after all danger of frost. Cover seeds with soil or planting medium according to package directions. For continuous bloom, deadhead spent flower stalks. Avoid taller varieties, which grow on spindly stems and are not generally satisfactory for windy seaside environments. Flowers possess an evocative clove fragrance known to drive gentle persons into frenzies of passion.

♣ *Dyssodia tenuiloba* (Dahlberg daisy)
Bright yellow daisylike flowers. 12″. Thrives in full sun, in ordinary, sandy soil. Drought resistant. Start indoors under lights eight weeks before last frost date in your area according to package instructions. Plants take four months to bloom from seed. Deadhead for continuous bloom.

♣ *Eschscholtzia californica* (California poppy)
Yellow, orange, cream, pink, or soft rose silky blossoms. Smooth, gray-green foliage. 12″. Thrives in full sun, in ordinary, sandy soil. Drought resistant. Surface sow outdoors after all danger of frost. Do not cover seeds with soil or planting medium since light is needed for germination. For continuous

bloom, deadhead spent blossoms. A nearly indestructible plant for difficult seaside environments.

♣ *Gaillardia* (Blanket flower)
Large red daisylike blossoms with yellow-tipped petals. 12–24″. Thrives in full sun, in ordinary well-drained soil. Drought resistant. Start indoors under lights six weeks before last frost date in your area or sow in situ after all danger of frost. Do not cover seeds with soil or planting medium since some light is needed for germination. There are also perennial varieties.

♣ *Glaucium corniculatum* (Sea poppy)
Large red or yellow poppylike blossoms, often with black centers. Bold, green foliage. To 18″. Thrives in full sun, in sandy soil. Drought resistant. Sow in situ, 1/4″ deep, after all danger of frost. For continuous bloom deadhead spent blossoms. Self-seeds freely once established.

♣ *Gypsophila elegans* (Baby's breath)
Tiny clusters of white or pink blossoms. Medium green lance-shaped foliage. 12–24″. Thrives in full sun, in ordinary soil. Drought resistant. Sow outdoors after all danger of frost. Barely cover seeds as some light is necessary for germination. G. *paniculata* is the perennial species. Excellent as a backdrop for an annual garden, although some staking will be necessary in windy environments.

♣ *Helianthus* (Sunflower)
Yellow or white daisy-shaped blossoms. Medium-green foliage. Suitable dwarf varieties grow to from 12–24″. Thrives in full sun, in ordinary soil. Drought resistant. Sow outdoors after all danger of frost. Cover seeds with soil or planting medium according to package directions. For continuous bloom, deadhead spent flower stalks. Use only the lesser known, dwarf varieties for seaside plantings, unless you have a sunny, sheltered area where taller varieties (to 10′) won't get knocked over by the wind.

♣ *Helichrysum* (Strawflower)
Daisy-shaped blossoms in a wide range of colors. Medium-green foliage. 12–24″. Thrives in full sun, in ordinary soil. Drought resistant. Start indoors under lights six weeks before last frost date in your area. Cover seeds with soil or planting medium according to package directions. Plant seedlings

outdoors after all danger of frost. Deadheading is not necessary. Stalks of flowers can be dried and used in arrangements.

Heliotropium (Heliotrope)
Clusters of deep-purple florets. Compact, bushy, deep-green or bronze foliage. 8–12″. Thrives in full sun and enriched soil. Needs some moisture. Start indoors under lights six to eight weeks before last frost date in your area. Cover seeds with soil or planting medium according to package directions. Plant seedlings outdoors after all danger of frost. For continuous bloom, deadhead spent flower stalks. This old-fashioned favorite is highly fragrant, scenting the garden particularly in the evening. Strangely enough, it rarely is grown in American gardens. *H. curassavicum* (seaside heliotrope) is tolerant of salt spray.

Impatiens
Pink, white, coral, salmon, red, magenta, purple, or orange blossoms. Deep-green foliage. 12–24″, depending on variety. Thrives in semi or deep shade in enriched soil. Needs some moisture. Start indoors under lights six to eight weeks before last frost date in your area. Surface sow. Do not cover seeds with soil or planting medium since light is needed for germination. Plant seedlings outdoors after all danger of frost. It is not necessary to deadhead. The tried and true flowering plant for shady areas.

Impatiens Balsamina (Garden balsam)
Pink, white, coral, red, peach, and lavender spikes of blossoms. Deep-green foliage. 24–36″. Thrives in partial shade or deep shade in enriched soil. Needs some moisture. Start indoors under lights six to eight weeks before last frost date in your area. Surface sow. Do not cover seeds with soil or planting medium since light is needed for germination. Plant seedlings outdoors after all danger of frost. It is not necessary to deadhead. A good companion for *Impatiens* in shady areas. Self-seeds freely in many areas.

Lantana
Lantana is not technically an annual, but a tropical and subtropical plant that can be easily wintered over indoors and is excellent for seaside porches and patios in pots or hanging baskets. Masses of small flowers in white, pink, yellow, or red. Dark

green leathery leaves. Must have lots of sun to flower, but tolerates sandy soil, wind, and salt spray. Water occasionally during summer drought.

Lobelia Erinus (Edging lobelia)
Intense blue, purple, burgundy, or white clusters of blossoms, some with white eyes. Mounded, fragile, medium-green foliage. 8″. Thrives in partial shade, but will blossom in partial sun, in sandy soil. Needs some moisture. Start indoors under lights six to eight weeks before last frost date in your area. Surface sow. Do not cover seeds with soil or planting medium since light is needed for germination. Plant seedlings outdoors after all danger of frost. It is not necessary to deadhead. Cascading varieties, such as 'Blue Cascade' are spectacular in hanging baskets. If mound-form 'Crystal Blue' is too intense for your scheme, use 'Cambridge Blue,' a paler shade. See under perennials for other *Lobelia* species.

♣ Lobularia maritima (Sweet alyssum)
White, rose, or purple florets. Mounded medium-green foliage. 4–8″. Thrives in full sun or partial shade in well-drained soil. Drought resistant. Surface sow in situ, after all danger of frost. Do not cover seeds with soil or planting medium since light is needed for germination. Be patient as germination can be slow. A tough plant ideally suited to a seaside environment. Self-seeds freely once established.

Matthiola (Stock)
Well-formed spikes of double florets in violet, lavender, rose, red, or white. Handsome medium-green foliage. 10–18″. Thrives in full sun and ordinary soil. Needs some moisture. Start indoors under lights six to eight weeks before last frost date in your area. Surface sow. Do not cover seeds with soil or planting medium since light is needed for germination. Plant seedlings outdoors after all danger of frost. For continuous bloom, deadhead spent flower stalks. An old-fashioned, heavily fragrant plant that (like the similar wallflower, *Cheiranthus Cheiri*) is rarely grown in American gardens. Select from dwarf varieties as taller types must be staked to protect from wind damage.

♣ Moluccella laevis (Bells of Ireland)
Greenish-yellow spikes of bell-shaped florets. Medium-green foliage. 24–36″. Thrives in full sun,

in ordinary soil. Drought resistant. Start indoors under lights eight weeks before last frost. Barely cover seeds with planting medium.Plant seedlings outdoors after all danger of frost. It is not necessary to deadhead. Unusual green blossoms add an exotic touch to the garden.

Nicotiana (Tobacco plant)
Predominantly white, but also red, pink, yellow, and purple star-shaped blossoms. Coarse medium-green foliage. 24–48″. Thrives in full sun, in ordinary soil. Needs some moisture. Start indoors under lights six weeks before last frost date in your area. Surface sow. Do not cover seeds with soil or planting medium since light is needed for germination. Plant seedlings outdoors after all danger of frost. For continuous bloom, deadhead spent flower stalks. Very fragrant, with a tobacco scent. Some varieties bloom at night.

♣ Nigella (Love-in-a-mist)
Spidery blue, purple, pink, or white, blossoms. Medium-green foliage. To 24″. Thrives in full sun, in well-drained soil. Drought resistant. Sow outdoors, in situ, 1/16th inch deep, after all danger of frost. This old favorite has recently been rediscovered by many gardeners. A tough old bird, it's blossoms can be dried and used in flower arrangements.

Pelargonium X domesticum (Zonal geranium)
This is the standard garden geranium, used throughout the world to decorate patios. Bright red, pink, or white flowers. Coarse, hairy leaves with rings of color. To 24″ Thrives in full sun and ordinary soil. Water during long summer drought. Start indoors under lights six weeks before last frost date in your area according to package instructions, root from cuttings taken from houseplants, or purchase plants. P. peltatum (ivy-leaved geranium) is useful in hanging baskets and withstands wind.

Petunia
Scores of colors and combinations of colors of these trumpet shaped blossoms are available. Fuzzy, low-growing, medium-green foliage. Thrives in full sun, in enriched soil. Needs some moisture. Start indoors under lights eight weeks before last frost date in your area. Surface sow. Do not cover seeds with soil or planting medium since light is needed for germination. Plant seedlings outdoors after all danger of

frost. For continuous bloom, it is very important to deadhead spent flower blossoms and stalks. Select heat-resistant varieties for seaside gardens. I recommend the single-flowered F1 hybrids of the variety often called P. multiflora in catalogues. Suitable for container plantings or hanging baskets.

♣ Phlox
Buff, pink, salmon, red, blue, purple, orange, or yellow clusters of blossoms. Attractive medium-green foliage. 7–12″. Thrives in full sun, in ordinary soil. Drought resistant. Sow seeds in situ outdoors, after all danger of frost. Cover seeds with soil or planting medium according to package directions. For continuous bloom, deadhead spent flower stalks. Easy to grow and available in a wider color range than perennial phlox.

♣ Portulaca
Single and double red, pink, yellow, orange, salmon, coral, or white blossoms. Succulent, sprawling foliage. 6″. Thrives in full sun, in sandy soil. Drought resistant. Surface sow outdoors after all danger of frost. Do not cover seeds with soil or planting medium since light is needed for germination. It is not necessary to deadhead. An ideal seaside plant and container plant, as the succulent leaves store water.

Salpiglossis sinuata (Painted tongue, velvet flower)
Red, purple, brown, yellow, and cream, funnel-shaped, velvety blossoms, often veined with gold. Medium-green foliage. To 30″. Thrives in full sun and enriched soil. Needs some moisture. Start indoors under lights twelve weeks before last frost date in your area. Cover seeds with soil or planting medium according to package directions. Plant seedlings outdoors after all danger of frost. For continuous bloom, deadhead spent flower stalks. An offbeat flower to use in arrangements. Often self-seeds in milder climates.

Salvia (Sage)
Brilliant red and purple spikes of florets. Handsome, dark-green foliage. 12–48″, depending on variety. Thrives in full sun, in ordinary soil. Needs some moisture. Surface sow outdoors, after all danger of frost. Do not cover seeds with soil or planting medium since light is needed for germination. When

plants are 3–4″ high, pinch tops to encourage branching and, thus, more flowers. For continuous bloom, deadhead spent flower stalks. Be aware that *Salvia* colors are very vivid and considered garish by many. *Salvia farinacea* 'Victoria' is much in favor, as it is always easier to integrate purples into a garden scheme than bright reds. Perennial sage is listed under "Herbs."

Scabiosa (Pincushion flower)

Ball-shaped blue, white, rose, pink, salmon, crimson, or lavender blooms. Medium-green foliage. 3′ Thrives in full sun, in ordinary soil. Needs some moisture. Sow outdoors, in situ, after all danger of frost. Cover seeds with soil or planting medium according to package directions. For continuous bloom, deadhead spent flower stalks. Easy to grow and rarely seen in American gardens.

♣ Statice

Apricot, rose, purple, deep blue, light blue, white, or yellow sprays of florets. Medium-green foliage. 24–30″. Thrives in full sun, in ordinary soil. Drought resistant. Start indoors under lights eight weeks before last frost. Barely cover seeds with planting medium. Plant seedlings outdoors after all danger of frost. It is not necessary to deadhead. Blossoms can be dried and used in flower arrangements.

♣ Senecio Cineraria (Dusty miller)

Stunning silver foliage. 8″–12″. Compact, mound-like growth habit. No flowers. Thrives in full sun, in ordinary well-drained soil. Drought resistant. Start indoors under lights six weeks before last frost date in your area. Cover seeds with soil or planting medium according to package directions. Plant seedlings outdoors after all danger of frost. Also called *Cineraria maritima*. An ideal seaside garden plant, native to a seaside environment. Silver foliage can be used effectively to set off blue and pale yellow flowering plants.

Tagetes (Marigold)

Gold, yellow, orange, white, or maroon single or double pompon blossoms. Deep-green foliage. 6–48″, depending on variety. Thrives in full sun, in ordinary soil, but will bloom in partial shade. Needs some moisture. Sow outdoors, after all danger of frost. Cover seeds with soil or planting medium

according to package directions. For continuous bloom, deadhead spent flower stalks. Tried and true, easy to grow, a perfect plant for a seaside environment. If vivid oranges and golds are not to your liking, select from recently introduced white and cream colored varieties. Taller varieties may need staking in unprotected areas.

♣ Tithonia rotundifolia (Mexican sunflower)

Large scarlet-orange, yellow-centered dahlialike blossoms. Medium-green foliage. 30–36″. Thrives in full sun, and in ordinary soil. Drought resistant. Surface sow outdoors, after all danger of frost. Do not cover seeds with soil or planting medium since light is needed for germination. For continuous bloom, deadhead spent flower stalks.

Verbena

Red, pink, lilac, yellow, or white blossoms, often with white eyes, on large trusses. Medium-green foliage. Often fragrant. *Verbena* has a tendency to spread, with one plant covering a considerable amount of space by the end of the season. Thrives in full sun and ordinary soil. Needs some moisture. Start indoors under lights eight weeks before last frost date in your area. Cover seeds with soil or planting medium according to package directions. Plant seedlings outdoors after all danger of frost. For continuous bloom, deadhead spent flower stalks.

Zinnia

Blooms come in all colors except blue and range in size from miniatures to giants. Deep-green foliage. 8–48″. Thrives in full sun, in ordinary soil. Needs some moisture. Sow outdoors after all danger of frost. Cover seeds with soil or planting medium according to package directions. For continuous bloom, deadhead spent flower stalks. When seedlings are 4″ high, pinch tips to encourage branching and thus, more flowers. Zinnias are prone to mildew, which can make them look unsightly, but there is some evidence that light salt spray increases their resistance. Newly hybridized varieties resist mildew.

Bulbs

SPRING BULBS

Hardiness: All of these spring-blooming bulbs are hardy as far north as Zone 3, and should be planted in the fall.

Allium (Ornamental onion)

True bulbs. Round or flat flower heads and onion-like foliage. See page 126 for colors and heights.

Anemone blanda (Greek anemone)

Rhizomes. Bluish-purple, pink, red, or white daisy-like blossoms. Medium-green, leafy foliage. 4–6″. Plant 4–6″ deep, 3–4″ apart. Soak rhizomes in room temperature water for forty-eight hours before planting. The white variety is particularly effective when overplanted with Red Riding Hood tulips.

Chionodoxa Luciliae (Glory-of-the-snow)

True bulbs. Blue, pink, or white star-shaped blooms. Spearlike, medium-green foliage. 4–5″. Plant 3″ deep, 1–3″ apart. Easy to grow. *Chionodoxa* multiply readily into substantial clumps.

Convallaria majalis (Lily of the valley)

True bulbs. Familiar, bell-shaped, fragrant white or pink blossoms. Broad, medium-green foliage. 8″. Plant 3″ deep, 3–4″ apart. These old-fashioned favorites are very easily grown and beyond their charm, the foliage serves as an excellent, non-invasive ground cover in shady areas.

Crocus

Corms. Gold, yellow, orange, lemon, light blue, lavender, purple, white, cream, or plum-colored goblet-shaped blossoms. Medium-green grasslike foliage. Plant 2″ deep, 1″ apart. See page 126 for recommended species and varieties.

Crocus vernus (Dutch crocus)

Corms. Familiar deep-purple, white, yellow, or lilac goblet-shaped blossoms. Medium-green grasslike foliage. 4–6″. Plant 3″ deep, 3–6″ apart. Good sea-side plant. Naturalizes when established.

Eranthis (Winter aconite)

Tubers. Bright yellow, small, buttercup-like blossoms on 2–4″ medium-green clusters of foliage. Plant 2″ deep, 3–4″ apart, as soon as they are available in late summer. Soak in tepid water for twenty-four hours before planting. The most common cause of failure is late planting: the longer tubers sit on shelves or in your house, the drier they get and the less likely they are to grow. Along with *Galanthus*, the earliest of all the spring-blooming bulbs, often growing right through the snow. And, if conditions are right, they will self-sow and naturalize.

Fritillaria imperialis (Crown imperial)

True bulbs. Red, orange, or yellow clusters of blossoms. Erect clusters of straplike foliage. 30–48″. Plant 8″ deep, 8″ apart. The blossoms do not smell pleasant, so they are best kept away from dooryards or windows. All animals hate them.

Fritillaria Meleagris (Guinea hen flower)

True bulbs. Purple and white or white drooping, bell-shaped blossoms, with checkered pattern. Grasslike foliage. 12″. Plant 3–4″ deep, 3–4″ apart. Plants often naturalize once established.

Fritillaria Michailovskyi (Michael's flower)

True bulbs. Bronze-maroon, yellow-edged, bell-shaped blossoms. Straplike foliage. 8–12″. Plant 3–4″ deep, 3–4″ apart. This charming and interesting species has only recently become available through mail-order nurseries in the United States and Canada.

Galanthus (Snowdrop)

True bulbs. Translucent, white, bell-shaped blossoms. Slender medium-green foliage. Plant 2–3″ deep, 2–3″ apart. Along with *Eranthis*, the earliest blooming of all the spring bulbs. Once planted, leave them where they are, since each year the bloom display will become more and more lush and dramatic.

Hyacinthus orientalis (Dutch hyacinth)

True bulbs. Blue, purple, red, pink, yellow, cream, white, or orange-peach columnar spikes of flowerlets. Jade-green, straplike foliage. 8–12″. Plant 5″ apart, 6″ deep. Familiar to all, hyacinths are easily grown in the garden. Their stiff appearance make it difficult to imagine using them effectively in most landscapes, but, after the first year of bloom, the stalks of flowerlets loosen up substantially, taking

Snowdrops

Sweet William and Hybrid Asiatic lilies

on a lovely, informal look. Their scent is unforgettable.

Iris Danfordiae
True bulbs. Yellow, iris-shaped blossoms. Grasslike foliage. 6″. Plant 3–4″ deep, 3–4″ apart. Although they rarely bloom a second year, these are worth the effort of planting every fall. Along with the *Iris*

reticulata, they provide sparkling, late winter color in a seaside garden.

Iris reticulata
True bulbs. Light blue, lavender, or purple, iris-shaped blossoms. Grasslike foliage. 6″. Plant 3–4″ deep, 3–4″ apart. This low-growing iris often blooms as early as late February. Coupled with *Iris Danfordiae*'s bright yellow blossoms, they certainly lift the late winter doldrums.

Iris, rhizomatous, see Perennials

Muscari (Grape hyacinth)
True bulbs. Bright blue, pale blue, or white clusters of blossoms. Sprawling, straplike foliage. 4–12″. Plant 3″ deep, 3″ apart. Most flowers of these charming bulbs resemble bunches of grapes. They perfume the surrounding air with a lovely, subtle sweet fragrance. See page 126 for recommended species and varieties.

121

Narcissus (Daffodil)
True bulbs. White, yellow, gold, orange, or apricot, and combinations thereof, depending on variety. There are eleven basic types of narcissus according to a system established by the Royal Horticultural Society of Great Britain and followed by bulb growers throughout the world. Shapes include the familiar trumpet, small-cupped, large-cupped, double, and so forth. All grow on erect 12–24″ stems over swordlike medium-green foliage. Plant 8″ deep, 6–8″ apart, depending on size of bulb. Daffodils are probably the most universally grown and loved of all the spring-flowering bulbs, for practical as well as esthetic reasons: they are not only pest and disease free, but rodent proof as well. Most varieties perform well for years. After about three years, some form thick clumps of foliage but steadily produce fewer flowers. If that happens, dig them after foliage withers, separate the bulbs and replant. See page 127 for recommended varieties.

Narcissus (Miniature daffodil)
True bulbs. Yellow, orange or white and combinations thereof. Trumpet-shaped or double blossoms on 6–14″ stalks, depending on variety, over medium green, spearlike foliage. Plant 4–6″ deep, 4–6″ apart. These mini-sized versions of the standard daffodils add great charm to dooryard gardens,

rockeries, and foundation plantings. Still, many gardeners have not yet discovered them. They are very reasonable in price and are a joy to behold in the spring. See page 128 for recommended varieties.

Puschkinia (Striped squill)
True bulbs. Bluish white or white clusters of ½–1″ blossoms on 4–8″ stalks over straplike foliage. Plant 3″ deep, 2–3″ apart. It will self-sow and naturalize if conditions are favorable. A bulb which should be more popular. This one is ideal for the spring garden, tucked here and there in the front of the border.

Scilla hispanica (Spanish bluebell)
True bulbs. Blue, white, or pink spiked clusters of 1″ bell-shaped blossoms on 12″ stalks over medium-green, straplike foliage. Plant 3–4″ deep, 6–8″ apart. These semi-tall growing bulbs should be planted more widely. They are ideal for naturalizing in areas of partial shade or in woodland gardens. I prefer the blue or white varieties rather than the pink, which has a washed out look when in bloom.

Scilla sibirica/Scilla Tubergeniana (Squill)
True bulbs. Brilliant blue, pale blue, lilac pink, or white, bell-shaped or star-shaped blossoms on 3–12″ stems over straplike leaves. Plant 3″ deep, 3–4″ apart. With sensationally beautiful electric blue blossoms, *Scilla sibirica* is perhaps my favorite early spring-blooming bulb. The blossoms of *Scilla Tubergeniana* are pale blue or white and although charming, do not make the visual impact of the *sibiricas*.

Tulipa (Tulip)
In Holland, and indeed throughout Europe, most gardeners treat tulips as annuals; that is, they plant them in fall and then, after bloom, dig them up and throw them away. They do this because they know that most tulips produce fewer and fewer blooms with each passing year. Here in America, however, we tend to think in terms of permanent, perennial plantings, so we plant tulips and then, several years down the line, wonder why they are no longer producing spectacular bloom. The reason is that tulip bulbs divide into small bulbs each year, and if the planting is not fertilized and the soil structure and climate are not ideal, they deplete. Even under optimal conditions, the blooms usually become smaller and smaller, eventually disappearing.

Therefore in your garden, most tulips cannot be counted on after a year or two. Some varieties are more prone to "perennialize" than others —that is, to provide a continuing display year after year—but they must be fertilized properly to achieve this effect. Beyond this, conditions vary to such an extent from area to area, from garden to garden, and even within an individual garden, that you cannot count on true perennialization of tulips.

There are many types of tulips available. Species tulips, most of which are the earliest to bloom and the closest genetically to the original wild tulips, include *T. Kaufmanniana*, *T. Fosterana* (the so-called emperor tulips), and *T. Greigii*. All of these tend to perennialize and multiply, providing beautiful displays year in and year out. Early-blooming triumph tulips, later blooming cottage, Rembrandt, parrot, lily-flowered, and viridiflora tulips, and the hundreds of varieties of Darwin tulips are not prone to perennialize, usually producing less and less bloom each year. The spectacular Darwin hybrids, a cross between *T. Fosterana* and the Darwin tulip, does tend to perennialize if conditions are favorable. I have a planting of Darwin hybrid Golden Apeldoorn now in its sixth year, more beautiful and with more blooms than when it was planted.

In addition to the above, there is a class of wild or near-wild tulips that truly does perennialize. Small in stature and bloom, these tulips usually multiply freely and can be used in rock gardens, door yard gardens, or anywhere they can be viewed closely. Most are early bloomers and are available from mail-order sources.

T. Kaufmanniana
Salmon, scarlet, yellow, cream, apricot, orange and combinations thereof. Tulip-shaped and water-lily shaped blossoms on 6–12″ erect stems over medium-green, medium-green and burgundy, or medium-green and white foliage. Plant 6″ deep, 3–6″ apart. These are much lower growing than the Dutch hybrids and Darwins, but are well-suited to seaside gardens. See page 128 for recommended varieties.

T. Greigii
Orange, red, yellow, gold, cream pink, ivory and combinations thereof. Tulip-shaped and water-lily

shaped blossoms on 6–20″ erect stems over medium green foliage usually mottled with purple or brown. Plant 6″ deep, 3–6″ apart. Generally larger than *T. Kaufmanniana.* See page 129 for recommended varieties.

T. Fosterana (Emperor tulip)
Red, pink, yellow, white, orange and combinations thereof. 4″, turban-shaped blossoms on 12–20″ stems over medium-green or medium-green and purple, broad-leafed foliage. Plant 6″ deep, 4–6″ apart. These are early blooming, tall tulips which tend to perennialize. Until recently only solid colors were available, but each year, hybridizers are creating new and interesting varieties which are being offered to gardeners. See page 129 for recommended varieties.

T. species
Yellow, white, red, rose, purple, or combinations thereof. 1–2″, tulip-shaped blossoms on erect 3–18″ stems over broad, medium-green foliage, some twisted. Plant 3–4″ deep, 3–4″ apart. If these irresistible, early-blooming miniature tulips are happy, they will multiply as they do in nature. They are certainly worth trying to see if they become established. See page 129 for recommended varieties.

Tulip, Dutch
All colors except blue. Turban-shaped single or double blooms on 18–36″, erect stems over medium-green, broad-leafed foliage, depending on variety. Plant 8–12″ deep, 6″ apart. There are a number of classifications of tulips beyond the species listed above. These bloom throughout the spring, and if you select from each category, you can have around two months of tulip bloom. In a seaside environment, treat them as annuals, digging and discarding them after bloom. Install new plantings each fall. Just to sift things out for you, here are the various classifications according to bloom time:
Early spring: Single early, Double early.
Mid-spring: Mendel, Triumph, Darwin hybrid, Double peony, *Viridiflora.*
Late spring: Darwin, Lily-flowered, Cottage, Rembrandt, Parrot, Double late.

SUMMER BULBS
Hardiness: Except for lilies, the following bulbs are tender and must be planted in the spring, after all danger of frost, rather than in the fall. They must be dug in the fall, after foliage has withered or been killed by frost, dried, cleaned and then stored over the winter in dry peat moss or vermiculite in a cool, dry, dark place. They can be replanted in the spring. Treat lilies like hardy perennials.

Acidanthera bicolor (Abyssinian gladioli, peacock orchid)
Corms. Creamy white, mahogany-centered, 2″ star-shaped blossoms on 18–24″ spearlike, medium-green foliage. Plant in full sun or partial shade, in ordinary soil, in spring, after all danger of frost, 3″ deep, 4″ apart. Scratch a light dusting of 5-10-5 fertilizer into soil when leaves emerge and again three or four weeks later. Stake plants when 1′ high. Water during summer drought. If you are north of Zone 6, it is easier to buy new corms, which are quite inexpensive, than to winter corms over. The blossoms exude a heavy, provocative perfume, more pronounced during the torpid heat of midsummer evenings.

Canna (Canna lily)
Rhizomes. Red, orange, yellow, pink, cream, white, or bicolored, 4–5″ blossoms on 18″–6′ spikes over broad, bright green, blue-green, or bronze leaves, depending on variety. Plant in full sun, in ordinary soil, in spring, after all danger of frost, ½″ deep, 15–18″ apart. Scratch a light dusting of 5-10-5 fertilizer into soil every two weeks during growing season. Water during summer drought. North of Zone 7, cut the stalks to the ground after they are blackened by frost, dig roots, and dry in an airy, shady, frost-free place for a few days. Store the rhizomes upside down in dry peat moss, perlite, or vermiculite, and replant in the spring. Be very careful in selecting the varieties that you wish to grow, as even a small planting will overwhelm almost any garden. The most wind resistant are the dwarf varieties (Pfitzer Hybrids, Seven Dwarfs), which are also more in scale for the average garden. Although the screaming reds, oranges, and yellows look inviting in garden catalogues and are even attractive in large public parks, the more subdued pinks, creams, and whites are far more suitable for a seaside home garden.

Crocosmia (Montbretia)
Corms. Yellow, orange, or scarlet 1½″ blooms on 24–48″ stalks with spearlike, medium-green foliage.

Plant in full sun, in ordinary soil, in spring, after all danger of frost, 3″ deep, 4″ apart. Scratch a light dusting of 5-10-5 fertilizer into soil when plants emerge and also three or four weeks later. Stake plants when one foot high. North of Zone 7, order and plant new corms each spring.

Gladiolus

Corms. Blossoms in every color of the rainbow on 1–5′ stalks with medium-green, spearlike foliage. Plant in full sun, in sandy soil, in spring, after all danger of frost, 6″ deep, 5″ apart. Scratch a light dusting of 5-10-5 fertilizer into soil when plants emerge and also 3–4 weeks later. Stake plants when 1′ high. Water during summer drought. North of Zone 7, order and plant new corms each spring. Because they are very stiff in appearance, I have found that selecting the dwarf varieties and planting them in a clump, allowing them to flop over, softens gladioli's harsh growth habit and adds an interesting touch of informality to this flower usually associated with funerals.

Lilium (Lily)

True bulbs. All colors except blue. Depending on variety, 4–8″ star or trumpet-shaped blossoms, on 2–7′ stalks with glossy, dark-green leaves. Plant in full sun to partial shade in enriched soil. Set bulbs 6–8″ deep, with small lily bulbs 6″ apart and larger bulbs (those the size of a fist) 18″ apart. Stake taller varieties stalks as they grow, but be careful not to drive stake too close to stalk as you might injure the bulb. Shorter varieties, such as Hybrid Asiatic Lilies, usually do not need staking. Lilies are among the few hardy summer flowering bulbs, and they do not have to be dug in fall and stored indoors over the winter. You can use lilies in perennial borders and island beds, for masses of color among shrub borders, or incorporated within foundation plantings. A bonus is that lilies attract hummingbirds. These are the available cultivars:

Aurelian hybrids: These are the towering trumpet lilies that can grow to 8′. They look magnificent as a backdrop for a very wide border, but for most seaside plantings they are too tall.

Hybrid Asiatics: These are much more manageable and sensible for the seaside landscape than the Aurelian hybrids, as they grow to between 2′ and 4′, depending on the variety. The flower spike is compact with many blooms, some in solid colors, others speckled. Be very careful when selecting colors, as some can be quite startling, even garish.

L. speciosum (Japanese lily): Many consider these the most beautiful of all the lilies. Colors are pink, rose, or white and combinations thereof. Although they can grow to 5′, they rarely need staking.

L. lancifolium (Tiger lily): Most of these varieties are spotted, with the petals turned back. Each produces from twelve to twenty flowers per stem. They reach a height of 3–4′. Here again, be careful in your color selection, as some varieties tend to be garish.

Polianthes tuberosa (Tuberose)

Rhizome. White, 2″ single or double blossoms on 15–24″ stems, with medium-green straplike foliage. Plant in full sun, in enriched soil in spring, after all danger of frost, 3″ deep, 6″ apart. Scratch a light dusting of 5-10-5 fertilizer into soil one month after leaves emerge, and every four weeks thereafter. North of Zone 7, order and plant new rhizomes each spring. Although foliage is rangy and blossoms are only mildly attractive, tuberose scent is so captivating that you might wish to consider growing them in your seaside garden.

Tigridia Pavonia (Tiger flower, Mexican shell flower)

True bulb. White, yellow, orange, scarlet, pink, lilac, buff, and combinations thereof. 5–6″ blossoms on 18–30″ stems with slightly untidy, spearlike foliage. Plant in full sun or partial shade, in ordinary soil, in spring, after all danger of frost, 6″ deep, 4–6″ apart. Scratch a light dusting of 5-10-5 fertilizer into soil once a month during growing season. North of Zone 7, order and plant new bulbs each spring. Although each flower lasts only one day, the many buds on each stalk create a display for many weeks.

Spring flowering bulbs

Winter aconite	Late winter
Snowdrop	Late winter/early spring
Crocus (Dutch)	Late winter/early spring
Crocus (Species)	Late winter/early spring
Iris Danfordiae	Late winter/early spring
Iris reticulata	Late winter/early spring
Glory-of-the-snow	Early spring
Puschkinia	Early spring
Scilla siberica	Early spring
Scilla tubergeniana	Early spring
Tulip, Greigii	Early/mid-spring
Tulip, Fosterana	Early/mid-spring
Tulip, Kaufmanniana	Early/mid-spring
Tulip, Species	Early/mid-spring
Anemone blanda	Early/mid-spring
Dutch hyacinth	Early/mid-spring
Daffodil and Narcissus (miniature)	Mid-spring
Fritillaria Meleagris	Mid-spring
Fritillaria Michailovskyi	Mid-spring
Fritillaria imperialis	Mid-spring
Grape hyacinth	Mid-spring
Daffodil and Narcissus (standard)	Mid-spring
Triumph tulip	Mid-spring
Double peony tulip	Mid-spring
Darwin hybrid tulip	Mid-spring
Lily-flowering tulip	Late spring
Darwin tulip	Late spring
Cottage tulip	Late spring
Parrot tulip	Late spring
Lily of the valley	Late spring
Allium	Late spring/early summer

Allium for the seaside garden

Variety	Color	Height
Allium giganteum	lavender	5–6'
A. elatum	violet	4–5'
A. Rosenbachianum	violet	4–5'
A. aflatunense	lavender	3–5'
A. atropurpureum	deep purple	30"
A. sphaerocephalum	deep purple	30"
A. Christophii	deep purple	18"
A. caeruleum	sky blue	18"
*A. roseum**	rose	12–14"
*A. Moly**	yellow	9–18"
*A. neapolitanum**	white	12"

*Useful for naturalizing

Crocuses for the seaside garden (all 4–6″)

Variety	Color
Blue Bird	Outer petals deep violet with white margin, inner petals white
C. ancyrensis (Golden Bunch)	Deep golden yellow
C. angustifolius (*C. susianus*)	Bronze gold
C. chrysanthus 'Advance'	Outer petals purple, inner petals lemon yellow
C. chrysanthus 'Blue Pearl'	Delicate blue
C. chrysanthus 'Canary Bird'	Orange cup with bronze spots
C. chrysanthus var. *fusco-tinctus*	Yellow with plum stripes
Cream Beauty	Cream white with dark markings
Lady Killer	Violet-purple with white margin
Ruby Giant	Pale lavender with darker margin
Sieberi Violet Queen	Amethyst violet
White Triumphator	White with blue veins

Muscari for the seaside garden

Variety	Color	Height
M. armeniacum	Blue clusters	4–8"
M. botryoides 'Album'	White clusters	4–8"
M. hybrid (Blue Spike)	Double blue clusters	10–12"
M. latifolium	Rich blue clusters	12–15"
M. comosum 'Plumosum' (Feather)	Reddish-purple featherlike plumes	6–8"

Daffodils for the seaside garden

In 1972, the Planting Fields Arboretum on Long Island held a daffodil planting trial. Two hundred different varieties of daffodils were planted and the number of flowers produced was tabulated each year. After ten years, some varieties were still flowering to perfection; others had fewer flowers; still others had disappeared completely. Among the varieties that consistently produced a lavish display were the following.

Variety	Color	Height
Arctic Gold	Yellow	18″
Binkie	Yellow and white	12″
Campanile	Yellow and orange	14″
Carlton	Yellow	18″
Cherie	White and pink	12″
Dove Wings	Yellow with yellow	8″
Duke of Windsor	White and yellow-orange	18″
February Gold	Bright yellow and yellow	10″
Flower Record	White and white-orange	18″
Ice Follies	White with pale yellow	18″
March Sunshine	Yellow	9″
Mrs. R. O. Backhouse	White and pink	18″
Red Rascal	Yellow and red	18″
Spellbinder	Yellow and white	20″
Sweetness	Yellow	12″
Sun Chariot	Yellow and orange	20″
Thalia	Pure white	15″
Trevithian	Yellow	18″

Daffodil varieties that consistently produced a lavish display in the Netherlands Bulb Industry's four-year trials conducted at North Carolina State University included the following.

Variety	Color	Height
Barrett Browning	White and deep orange-red	20″
Brighton	Yellow	20″
Carbineer	Yellow and orange	18″
February Gold	Bright yellow and yellow	10″
Fortune	Yellow and orange	18″
Flower Record	White and white-orange	18″
Gigantic Star	Yellow	18″
Ice Follies	White and pale yellow	20″
Jumblie	Yellow and orange	9″
Salome	White and apricot-orange	15″
Sugarbush	White and yellow	12″
Tahiti	Yellow and orange-red	18″
Thalia	Pure white	15″
Trevithian	Yellow	18″

Miniature daffodils for the seaside garden

Variety	Color	Height
April Tears	Deep yellow	6–8″
Baby Moon	Buttercup yellow	9″
Double Jonquil	Double, bright yellow	10″
February Gold	Bright yellow and lemon	8″
Gold Drops	Yellow and white	10″
Hawera	Creamy yellow	8″
Hoop Petticoat	Bright yellow	6″
Jack Snipe	White and yellow	8″
Liberty Bells	Clusters of yellow	8″
Lintie	Yellow with orange rim	9″
Little Witch	Deep yellow	6″
Peeping Tom	Golden yellow	8″
Pipit	Sulphur and white	9″
Rip Van Winkle	Double clear yellow	6″
Suzy	Yellow and orange	14″
Tete-a-Tete	Yellow	8″

Kaufmanniana tulips for the seaside garden

Variety	Color	Height
Ancilla	Pink and white	6″
Chopin	Lemon yellow	6″
Fritz Kreisler	Salmon-pink	6″
Gold Coin	Scarlet-edged yellow	6–8″
Heart's Delight	Carmine and rose	10″
Kaufmanniana	Cream, yellow center	6″
Shakespeare	Salmon-orange-apricot	6–8″
Show Winner	Scarlet	6–8″
Stresa	Gold, orange border	7″
Vivaldi	Yellow and crimson	7″
Waterlily	Cream and carmine	7″

Greigii tulips for the seaside garden

Variety	Color	Height
Cape Cod	Orange-red, yellow inside	12–14″
Engadin	Yellow-edged deep red	12″
Lovely Surprise	Gold and red	18″
Oriental Splendor	Lemon-edged carmine red	20″
Plaisir	Cream-edged carmine red	12″
Red Riding Hood	Brilliant scarlet	6–8″
Royal Splendor	Scarlet	20″
Scheherazade	Scarlet	12″
Sweet Lady	Soft pink and ivory	8″

Fosterana (Emperor) tulips for the seaside garden

Variety	Color	Height
Concerto	Pure white	16″
Easter Parade	Carmine-rose, yellow inside	16″
Juan	Orange, yellow base	16″
Orange Emperor	Buttery orange	16″
Pink Emperor	Rose-pink	16″
Princeps	Bright red	16″
Red Emperor	Scarlet	16″
Sweetheart	Yellow edged white	16″
White Emperor (Purissima)	White	16″
Yellow Emperor	Golden yellow	16″

Species tulips for the seaside garden

Variety	Color	Height
Tulipa Bakeri 'Lilac Wonder'	Lilac and yellow	12″
T. biflora	Yellow and white	8″
T. chrysantha	Yellow and red	8″
T. Clusiana (Lady tulip, peppermint tulip)	Rose and white	8″
T. dasystemon (T. tarda)	Yellow and white	3–6″
T. Hageri	Deep red	6″
T. patens (Persian tulip)	Yellow and white	6–9″
T. praestans	Pale red	12–18″
T. pulchella	Pale purple	4–6″
T. turkestanica	White with yellow center	8″

Perennials

All of the entries are hardy to Zone 5 unless noted otherwise.

Astilbe Thunbergii, Malva moschata 'Alba,' *Lythrum salicaria* 'Morden's Pink', *Ajuga reptans* 'Burgundy Glow', *Sedum* 'Rosy Glow' and *Geranium sanguineum* var. *prostratum.*

♣ *Achillea* (Yarrow)
Yellow, white, pink, and red flower clusters on erect stalks with fernlike foliage. 24–48″. Thrives in ordinary soil in full sun. Drought resistant. Plant outdoors in spring or fall. Flowers are excellent for drying.

Aconitum (Monkshood)
Dark blue or blue and white spires of blossoms on 3–4′ stalks. Dark green, leafy foliage. Thrives in enriched soil, in partial shade or full sun. Needs moisture. Plant outdoors in mid-spring. Plant increases slowly and once established resents being moved. Monkshood is a good substitute for delphiniums.

Amsonia Tabernaemontana (Bluestar)
True blue clusters of upright or drooping blossoms and delicate, willowlike foliage. 12–36″. Thrives in enriched soil, in partial shade or shade. Needs moisture. Plant outdoors in mid-spring. Cut plants to ground after killing frost. Pruning after bloom helps maintain foliage, which turns brilliant yellow in fall.

Anemone X *hybrida* (Japanese anemone)
Pink, rose, or white blossoms with yellow centers. Medium-green foliage. 18–48″, depending on variety. Thrives in moderately fertile soil, in partial shade or full sun. Needs moisture. Plant outdoors in mid-spring or fall. Cut plants to ground after killing frost. Because they are late bloomers, Japanese anemones are particularly useful in the garden. Blossoms are delicate in appearance, which is rare for cultivars which bloom in the fall. Often sold as *Anemone japonica.*

♣ *Anthemis tinctoria* (Golden marguerite)
Yellow, daisylike, blossoms and gray-green, finely cut foliage. 18–24″. Thrives in ordinary soil in full sun. Drought resistant. Plant outdoors in mid-spring or fall. Deadhead throughout summer and fall to prolong blooming. Provides masses of flowers during the summer. In Tudor England, *Anthemis* was used for lawns, and when it was mowed, its fragrance, similar to chamomile, filled the air.

Aquilegia (Columbine)
Delicate, trumpetlike flowers in a full range of colors on delicate, often feathery, fernlike foliage. 18–36″. Thrives in enriched soil, in full sun or partial shade. Needs moisture. Plant outdoors in mid-spring or fall. Cut foliage to ground after killing frost. Delicate blossoms enhance the spring garden. Blue varieties are particularly beautiful.

♣ *Artemisia* (Perennial dusty miller)
Grown for silvery gray foliage. 12–36″, depending on variety. Thrives in enriched, well-drained, sandy soil in full sun. Drought resistant. Plant outdoors in mid-spring or late summer. Especially recommended for the seashore are A. *ludoviciana* var. *albula* 'Silver King,' 36″ and 'Silver Queen,' 24″. Also see *Artemisia* under groundcovers.

♣ *Asclepias tuberosa* (Orange butterfly weed)
Bright orange umbels of flowers in midsummer on bright green foliage. To 36″. Thrives in full sun and sandy soil. Drought resistant. Plants are late to break dormancy, so care must be taken not to dig them up mistakenly in spring. A. *incarnata*, a less familiar native, has pink and white flowers.

Astilbe
White, pink, red, rose, peach, or apricot feathery

Astilbe and gooseneck loosestrife (*Lysimachia clethroides*)

plumes of blossoms on sturdy, medium-green foliage. 12–30″. Thrives in moderately enriched soil, in partial shade or full sun. Needs moisture. Plant outdoors in mid-spring or fall. Remove spent blossoms after bloom cycle. Provides soft, feathery texture to the landscape.

♣ *Baptisia australis* (Wild blue indigo)
Indigo blue spikes of pealike blossoms over gray-green foliage. 3–4′. Thrives in enriched soil, in full sun. Drought resistant. Will grow in partial shade, but requires staking as plant can become rangy. Plant outdoors in mid-spring or fall.

♣ *Brunnera macrophylla* (Forget-me-not)
Sky blue, tiny forget-me-not-like blossoms on handsome, medium-green, heart-shaped foliage. 12–18″. Thrives in moderately fertile soil, in partial or deep shade. Drought resistant. Plant outdoors in mid-spring or fall. One of the few perennials which will thrive beneath the extensive surface root system of maples and beeches.

Chrysanthemum coccineum (Painted daisy)
White, pink, or red, and combinations thereof. Daisylike blossoms on medium-green foliage. 24″. Thrives in moderately fertile soil, in full sun or partial shade. Needs moisture. Plant outdoors in mid-spring or fall. Deadhead after bloom to encourage second flowering.

Chrysanthemum maximum (Shasta daisy)
White with yellow-centered, daisylike single or double blossoms on deep-green, handsome foliage. 12–42″. Thrives in moderately fertile soil, in full sun or partial shade. Needs moisture. Plant outdoors in mid-spring or fall. Deadhead after bloom to encourage second bloom.

♣ *Chrysanthemum* X *morifolium*
(Chrysanthemum)
Wide range of colors including yellow, gold, white, rust, orange, red, purple and lavender. Many blossom shapes, but pompon is perhaps the most readily available. Medium-green compact foliage, depending on variety. 8–36″. Thrives in moderately fertile soil, in full sun, but will tolerate partial shade. Drought resistant. Plant outdoors in mid-spring.

Montauk daisies bloom in the fall with the ornamental grasses. According to local lore, plants were washed up on the shores of Long Island many years ago when a ship carrying them from Japan sank off the coast.

Cut back foliage after killing frost. The following spring, dig plant, divide, discard woody center, and replant divisions. After planting, pinch shoots every three weeks until July 4 to encourage branching and thus more bloom.

♣ *Chrysanthemum nipponicum* (Montauk daisy)
White, daisylike blossoms with greenish-yellow centers on with deep green lustrous foliage. 3–5′. Thrives in ordinary, well-drained soil, in full sun to partial shade. Drought resistant. Plant outdoors in mid-spring. This is a fall-blooming perennial, and, as with all chrysanthemums, bloom must be thwarted for full effect, so shear entire plant to 1′ every two weeks starting in June. Do not shear after mid-August. A great favorite in Long Island seaside gardens.

♣ *Chrysopsis* (Golden aster)
Yellow, daisylike 2″ blossoms. 3–4′. Thrives in sandy soil, in full sun. Drought resistant. Plant outdoors in mid-spring or fall. Cut back to ground after frost.

Cimicifuga (Bugbane, snakeroot)
Plumelike white flower spikes bloom in late summer, over large leaves. 36–48″. Thrives in ordinary soil in sun or partial shade. Drought tolerant. Plant outdoors in mid-spring or fall. Can be rampantly invasive, spreading like wildfire by underground stolons. *C. racemosa* is native to the East Coast.

♣ *Coreopsis*
Yellow and yellow-mahogany-red, daisylike blossoms on medium-green, handsome foliage. 24″. Thrives in poor to ordinary soil, in full sun. Drought resistant. Plant outdoors in mid-spring or fall. Very easy to grow. If you want lots of carefree yellow flowers, this is a good choice.

♣ *Dianthus* (Pinks)
White, pink, or red or combinations thereof, single or double, carnation type blossoms on elegant, blue-green or gray-green foliage. 8–20″. Thrives in sandy soil, in full sun or partial shade. Drought resistant. Plant outdoors in mid-spring or fall. Deadhead after bloom to keep plant tidy. *D. barbatus* (sweet William) is a biennial or, at best, a short lived perennial, and seeds can be sown in August for bloom the following year. All pinks offer a lovely clovelike fragrance.

Dicentra spectabilis (Bleeding heart)
Pink or white heart-shaped blossoms on graceful, arching stems over medium-green foliage. 12–36″. Thrives in moderately fertile soil, in partial shade. Needs moisture. Plant outdoors in spring. Remove branches of spent blossoms after bloom to keep plant tidy. Foliage withers toward the end of summer, so an overplanting of annuals in the garden is recommended. Blooms with tulips, azaleas, and dogwood. Adds an air of graceful elegance to the spring garden.

Digitalis (Foxglove)
All colors except blue. Spikes of pitcher-shaped florets over medium-green rosettes of foliage. 18″–5′. Thrives in ordinary, well-drained soil, in partial shade or full sun. Needs moisture. Since foxglove is a biennial, start outdoors from seed after all danger of frost. Plant will not bloom first year, but will winter over and bloom second year. Once established, deadhead after bloom and it may flower again. Foxglove is easily grown from seed and may perennialize. If not, treat as a biennial.

Doronicum cordatum (Leopard's bane)
Yellow, daisylike, blossoms on handsome, deep-green foliage. 20″. Thrives in ordinary soil, in full sun or partial shade. Needs moisture. Plant outdoors in mid-spring or fall. Deadhead after bloom. Plant becomes semi-dormant after bloom so overplant with annuals in May or June. Leopard's bane is an early-blooming perennial used to contrast and soften spring bulb plantings.

♣ *Echinops* (Globe thistle)
Steel blue thistlelike blossoms on large-leafed, gray-green, hirsute foliage. 24–36″. Thrives in well-drained soil, in full sun. Drought resistant. Plant outdoors in mid-spring or fall. Divide plant only after three years.

♣ *Echinacea* (Purple coneflower)
Plum-pink or white, spidery 3″ blossoms with orange cone centers on handsome deep-green foliage. 3′. Thrives in sandy soil, in full sun. Drought resistant. Plant outdoors in mid-spring or fall. Deadhead spent blooms to encourage second bloom.

Eryngium
Steel blue, lacy, thistlelike blooms on thorny, hir-

sute foliage. 12–36″. Thrives in ordinary soil, in full sun. Needs moisture. Plant outdoors in mid-spring or fall. Deadhead after bloom. Taller varieties may need staking. *Eryngium maritimum* (sea holly), 12″, is naturalized along the East Coast and tolerates sandy soil.

Eupatorium coelestinum (Hardy ageratum)
Fluffy pale purple blossoms resembling annual ageratum on coarse hairy foliage. 36″. Thrives in well-drained soil, in full or partial sun. Needs moisture. Plant outdoors in mid-spring or fall. Plant benefits from pinching during season. This encourages sturdy branching and eliminates need for staking. *E. maculatum* (Joe-Pye weed), 2–6′, is an East Coast native found in damp areas and preferred by some gardeners to *E. coelestinum*.

Euphorbia epithymoides (Cushion spurge)
Bright yellow, chartreuse, and green clusters of florets and leaves combine over bright-green foliage. 12–18″. Thrives in ordinary soil, in full sun. Needs moisture. Plant outdoors in mid-spring or fall. Remove dead foliage after killing frost. Sap of plant is irritating to sensitive skin, causing a mild rash.

♣ *Gaillardia* (Blanket flower)
Yellow, red, or bicolored daisylike blossoms on handsome medium-green foliage. 12–30″. Thrives in ordinary soil, in full sun. Drought resistant. Plant outdoors in mid-spring or fall. Deadhead after bloom to keep plant tidy and to encourage more flowers.

♣ *Gaura Lindheimeri*
Tubular white flowers with pink tinge on hirsute, gray-green, willowy foliage. 4′. Thrives in enriched sandy soil, in full sun or partial shade. Drought resistant. Plant outdoors in mid-spring. Easily grown from seed. Deadhead for second bloom. Second year, when plant is about 1′ tall, cut back to 8″ to encourage bushy growth.

Gypsophila (Baby's breath)
White or pink sprays of tiny flowers on bushlike, graceful plants. 12–24″. Thrives in well-drained, fertile, alkaline soil, in full sun. Needs moisture. Plant outdoors in mid-spring or fall. Remove dead foliage after frost. Baby's breath lends a soft cloudlike quality to a perennial planting.

♣ *Heliopsis helianthoides* (Sunflower)
Golden yellow, double, pompon-shaped blossoms on medium-green foliage. 3–4′. Thrives in ordinary soil, in full sun. Drought resistant. Plant outdoors in mid-spring or fall. Deadhead after bloom to encourage second bloom.

♣ *Hemerocallis* (Daylily)
The familiar lily blossoms on 12–48″ stems over straplike medium green foliage. Thrives in ordinary soil, in full sun or partial shade. Drought resistant. Plant outdoors in mid-spring or fall. Foolproof and available in hundreds of varieties and colors to suit every landscape.

♣ *Heuchera sanguinea* (Coralbells)
Red, pink, or white spikes of small, bell-shaped blossoms over medium-green or variegated foliage. 12–18″. Thrives in moderately fertile, dry soil, in full sun or partial shade. Drought resistant. Plant outdoors in mid-spring or fall. Deadhead after bloom to keep plant tidy. Like baby's breath, the small florets of coralbells are useful for softening the perennial garden.

♣ *Hibiscus Moscheutos* (Rose mallow)
Flamboyant, pink, white, rose, fire-engine red and combinations thereof. 7–10″ blossoms over stunning lobed foliage. 3–6′. Thrives in enriched, well-drained soil, in full sun. Drought resistant. Plant in mid-spring, not in fall. Rose mallow is really a small shrub, although it is classified as an herbaceous perennial. If you want to make a startling statement in your garden, this plant is for you. *H. Moscheutos* subsp. *palustris* (marsh mallow), native to East Coast bogs, is pink.

Hosta (Plaintain lily)
White, lilac, or pale lavender delicate blossom spikes on lush foliage in colors ranging from yellow to dark green, gray, and near steel blue, often edged or speckled with white, cream, or yellow. Leaves can be smooth, ribbed, or quilted. 2–36″. *Hosta* will grow in just about any kind of soil and light conditions, but thrives in partial shade, in enriched, moist soil. Plant outdoors in mid-spring or fall. Remove spent blossoms after bloom to keep plant tidy. *Hosta* is an indispensable foliage plant. I favor 'Honeybells' (*H. plantaginea* X *H. lancifolia*), which has a light pleasing scent.

Iris Kaempferi (**Japanese iris**)
Blue, purple, white, or yellow and combinations thereof. Spear-shaped, medium-green foliage. To 24″. Thrives in wet soil, in full sun, but will tolerate partial shade. Plant outdoors in spring or fall. Many cultivars available. The closely related *I. laevigata* is a true bog plant and may perform even better in very wet soils. Adapts to wetland conditions.

Iris Pseudacorus (**Yellow flag iris**)
Light yellow to orange flowers over spear-shaped, medium-green foliage. To 5′. Naturalized on the East Coast and found in wet areas. Thrives in full sun, but will tolerate partial shade. Plant outdoors in spring or fall. Various cultivars available. Adapts to wetland conditions.

♣ *Iris siberica* (**Siberian iris**)
Blue, purple, white, or yellow and combinations thereof. Spear-shaped, medium-green foliage. 18–36″. Thrives in well-drained ordinary soil, in full sun, but will tolerate partial shade. Drought resistant. Plant outdoors in mid-spring or fall. Do not deadhead spent stalks as dried pods are attractive in a fall garden.

♣ *Iris,* **tall bearded**
The familiar bearded iris comes in a remarkable array of colors and heights. Foliage is jade-green, spearlike, and remains attractive throughout season. Thrives in enriched, well-drained soil, in full sun, but will tolerate partial shade. Drought resistant. Midsummer is the best time to plant bearded irises, but the fall will do. Remove spent stalks after bloom. Divide and replant every 3–5 years, depending on vigor of plant.

♣ *Kniphofia* (**Torch flower**)
Red and yellow pokerlike blooms over gray-green, grasslike foliage. 18–36″. Thrives in well-drained or sandy soil, in full sun. Drought resistant. Plant outdoors in mid-spring. Deadhead through season and shear foliage when it becomes rangy. Torch flower adds a tropical touch to the seaside garden.

♣ *Limonium latifolium* (**Sea lavender**)
Sprays of tiny lavender blossoms on spreading, silvery foliage. 24–36″. Thrives in well-drained, ordinary soil, in full sun. Drought resistant. Plant

outdoors in mid-spring. Easy to grow from seed. Sea lavender resembles baby's breath.

♣ *Linum* (**Flax**)
Sky blue or white small blossoms on willowy stems. 12–18″. Thrives in enriched, well-drained, soil, in full sun. Drought resistant. Plant outdoors in mid-spring. Easy to grow from seed. Sow in situ in mid-spring. Thin to 6″ apart when seedlings are established.

♣ *Lychnis Coronaria* (**Rose campion**)
Cerise or white blossoms on silver-gray, wooly textured foliage. 24–36″. Thrives in ordinary soil, in full sun. Drought resistant. Plant outdoors in mid-spring or fall. Deadhead after bloom to encourage new flowers.

♣ *Lythrum salicaria* 'Morden's Pink' (**Loosestrife**)
Tall spikes of purple or pink flowers on large bushes. 30–48″. Thrives in ordinary soil, in full sun or partial shade. Drought resistant. Loostrife can be invasive and is widely naturalized along the East Coast, but at least one, *L. salicaria* 'Morden's Pink,' a sterile variety that flowers all summer, is indispensable.

♣ *Malva moschata* (**Musk mallow, marsh mallow**)
Five-petalled, flamboyant, pink, white or red blossoms. 24–36″. Thrives in alkaline soil, in full sun or partial shade. Drought resistant. It reseeds profusely and can become a nuisance unless unwanted seedlings are removed. Deadhead after bloom to avoid problem.

Monarda (**Bee balm, bergamot, Oswego tea**)
Red, white, purple, or pink. 3″ whorls of petals on medium-green foliage. 24–48″. Thrives in ordinary soil, in full sun or partial shade. Needs moisture. Plant outdoors in mid-spring or fall. Deadhead after bloom. *Monarda* is subject to mildew, so plant in area where air circulation is good.

♣ *Oenothera tetragona* (**Evening primrose**)
Yellow, buttercup-like blossoms on elegant, medium-green, sometimes tinged with red, foliage. 12–24″. Thrives in well-drained, sandy soil, in full sun. Drought resistant. Plant in mid-spring. Spreads rapidly, but can be contained.

Paeonia (Peony)

Pink, coral, white, burgundy, red, yellow, and combinations thereof. Single or double pompon blossoms on lustrous, dark-green foliage which remains attractive throughout the season. Thrives in enriched soil, in full sun. 24–48″. Needs moisture. Plant outdoors in August or early September. Deadhead after bloom. Cut foliage to ground after killing frost, as disease can be harbored in foliage over winter.

♣ Perovskia (Russian Sage)

Powder blue spikes of tiny blossoms on delicate gray foliage. Thrives in enriched, well-drained soil, in full sun. Drought resistant. Plant outdoors in early spring. Cut back to 6″ in early spring. Practically indestructible.

♣ Papaver orientale (Oriental poppy)

White, scarlet, orange, pink, or peach, and combinations thereof. Large cup-shaped blossoms. 24–36″. Thrives in ordinary soil, in full sun. Drought resistant. Plant outdoors in early spring or fall. Remove foliage when it dries during midsummer. Plant goes dormant after flowering, so summer drought is rarely a problem. Overplant with annuals after bloom to cover the bare spot in the garden.

Phlox Paniculata (Perennial phlox)

White, pink, purple, red, lavender or orange, often with contrasting eye. Large flower heads composed of individual florets on stiff stalks with medium-green foliage. 4′. Thrives in enriched soil, in full sun but tolerates partial shade. Drought resistant. Plant outdoors in mid-spring or fall. Deadhead after bloom. Cut foliage to ground after killing frost. Phlox is subject to mildew, so plant in area where air circulation is good.

Platycodon (Balloon flower)

Purple, white or pink, balloon-shaped blossoms in spikes over medium-green foliage. 12–30″. Thrives in enriched soil, in full sun, but tolerates partial shade. Needs moisture. Plant outdoors in mid-spring or fall. Deadhead after bloom to encourage more flowers. Balloon flower is difficult to transplant because of its long taproot, but can be propagated from seed. Very dependable once established.

♣ Rudbeckia (Coneflower)

Gold, yellow, or rust-colored daisylike blossoms on medium-green foliage. 2–5′. Thrives in ordinary soil, in full sun. Drought resistant. Plant outdoors in mid-spring or fall. Deadhead after bloom to encourage new flowers. *R. hirta* is black-eyed Susan. Easy to grow, producing extravagant bloom.

♣ Saponaria officinalis (Bouncing Bet)

Pink or red clusters of double blossoms. 2–3′. Thrives in well-drained ordinary soil, in full sun. Sprawls all over in rich soil. Drought resistant. Plant anytime during the growing season. If plants get leggy in spring, trim back to encourage bushiness.

♣ Solidago (Goldenrod)

Golden, plumelike blossoms on medium-green foliage. 2–3′. Thrives in well-drained, ordinary soil, in full sun or part shade. Plant in mid-spring or sow seeds, in situ, in early spring. *S. sempervirens* (seaside goldenrod) is native to mid-Atlantic beaches and is a good dune binder in conjunction with American beach grass. Select *S. nemoralis, S. canadensis* or *S. Virgaurea* for gardens that are not directly on the ocean.

♣ Veronica (Speedwell)

Blue, lavender, white or pink spikes or clusters of blossoms on medium-green, lustrous foliage. 2–36″. Thrives in well-drained, sandy soil, in full sun, but tolerates partial shade. Drought resistant. Plant outdoors in early spring. Deadhead for repeat bloom.

♣ Verbena hastata (Blue vervain)

Blue flower spikes on coarse foliage. Drought resistant. Most gardeners would consider this native a weed, but it is a good soil binder on dunes, used in conjunction with American beach grass.

♣ Yucca

Large, bell-shaped, white or violet tinged blossoms, over rosettes of green or variegated swordlike foliage. 4–6′. Thrives in well-drained, sandy, poor soil, in full sun. Drought resistant. For occasional dramatic accents and a tropical look, nothing beats *Yucca*. But use it sparingly.

135

Herbs

Since most herbs are native to the dry areas of the Mediterranean and Middle East, where either sandy or very poor soil is the rule, they are an excellent choice for American seaside gardens. All cultivars included in this list are hardy throughout coastal areas of North America, except for the far northern reaches of Canada, and all are perennial, unless otherwise indicated.

Allium sativum (Garlic)
Bulb. Hardy, jade-green, spearlike foliage sporting purple clusters of blossoms in midsummer. To 36″. Prefers full sun and well-drained soil and is drought resistant, although regular watering during summer drought is advised. Plant bulbs in spring or fall. You can simply plant cloves of store-bought garlic. Elephant garlic, the giant, milder version, is available through mail-order sources. For larger bulbs, remove flower heads. In August, dig bulbs, clean, hang by their necks in dry place out of the sun until foliage is dry. Store bulbs in a refrigerator. Individual cloves can also be replanted after digging for the next year's crop.

♣ *Allium Schoenoprasum* (Chive)
Rhizome. Medium-green clumps of sparlike foliage sporting clusters of lavender blossoms in spring. 12″. Prefers full sun and well-drained soil. Drought resistant. Plant from seed anytime during the growing season. Chive self-seeds, so to avoid unwanted plants deadhead blossoms after flowering. An easily grown, indispensable kitchen herb, which is being used more and more for decorative landscape purposes.

♣ *Anethum graveolens* (Dill)
Annual. Feathery, medium-green foliage sporting seed heads of yellowish blossoms. To 36″. Prefers full sun and well-drained soil. Drought resistant. Plant from seed in spring after all danger of frost, and then again every three weeks for successive crops. An easily grown, indispensable kitchen herb. Feathery foliage can be worked into the landscape nicely.

♣ *Artemisia Abrotanum* (Southernwood)
Perennial. Lacy, grey-green leaves with small pale yellow blossoms. 24–48″. Prefers full sun and well-

drained soil. Drought resistant. Plant in spring after all danger of frost, and trim occasionally to keep plant tidy. Divide every 3–4 years. Foliage lasts from late spring to killing frost.

♣ *Artemisia Dranunculus* (French tarragon)
Perennial. Medium-green, glossy foliage. 12–36″. Prefers full sun and poor soil and resents water. Drought resistant. Plant in spring after all danger of frost. Carefree once established and handy in the kitchen.

Chamaemelum nobile (Chamomile)
Perennial. Low-growing, spreading plant with bright-green, soft-textured foliage. To 6″. Small, white-petaled, daisylike blossoms from late spring through summer. Apple-scented foliage. Thrives in sun to partial shade, in well-drained, ordinary soil. Water regularly during prolonged summer drought. A good selection for planting in walkways. Leaves can be dried and used to brew a refreshing tea.

♣ *Chrysanthemum Parthenium* (Feverfew)
Perennial. Light-green foliage sporting white, daisy-like flowers with yellow centers from midsummer to fall. 18–24″. Prefers full sun and sandy soil. Will also tolerate partial shade. Drought resistant. Plant in spring after all danger of frost. If conditions are favorable, feverfew will self-sow prodigiously. You can simply pull unwanted plants.

Galium odoratum (Sweet woodruff)
Perennial. Narrow, bright-green, aromatic foliage, with small white flowers in late spring and summer. 6–12″. Thrives in shade, in enriched soil. Requires regular moisture. Plant in spring after all danger of frost. Dried leaves can be used to flavor white wine. May wine is flavored with this herb.

Hyssopus officinalis (Hyssop)
Perennial. Smooth, narrow foliage, carrying small blue-violet blossom spikes in summer and fall. 18–24″. Hard to find are cultivars that sport white or pink blossoms. Prefers full sun and well-drained light soil and is drought resistant, but regular watering is recommended. Plant seeds, in situ, in spring, after all danger of frost. Self-sows if happy.

♣ *Lavandula* (Lavender)
Perennial. Narrow, silvery-gray, foliage, with white,

pink, or lavender spikes of tiny blossoms. 6–48″. Prefers full sun and ordinary soil. Drought resistant. Plant in spring after all danger of frost, or in fall. Among the varities recommended for seaside plantings are low-growing varieties of *L. angustifolia*, including 'Hidcote' (12″), 'Munstead' (18″), and 'Compacta' (10″). To keep plant tidy, shear after flowering.

♣ Mentha (Mint)
Perennial. There are many varieties of this familiar herb. Foliage is deep green, jade green, or purplish, with some varieties variegated in cream or yellow. Thrives in full sun and in ordinary soil. Drought resistant. Plant in spring after all danger of frost. Mint can become invasive if happy; plant it in containers that are sunk into earth to keep it from escaping.

♣ Nepeta (Catnip, catmint)
Perennial. Tiny, blue, lavender, yellow, or white sprays of tubular blossoms on medium-green foliage. 12–24″. Thrives in well-drained, ordinary soil, in full sun. Drought resistant. Plant outdoors anytime during the growing season. Catnip is an ideal border or edging plant for the seaside garden unless, perhaps, you have a cat. An intoxicated cat can obliterate a plant in no time flat.

Ocimum Basilicum (Basil)
Annual. The familiar kitchen herb, with foliage in deep green, bronze, or purplish green. 12–36″. Prefers full sun and ordinary soil and requires watering throughout season. Plant in situ, in spring, after all danger of frost. Look for new varieties, some dwarf and moundlike, many with purple or bronze foliage, and use in plantings for color effects.

Origanum vulgare (Oregano)
Perennial. Small, medium-green heart-shaped foliage. 24–30″. Some varieties have a sprawling growth habit. Greek oregano (*O. heracleoticum*) is neater, and more pungent. Thrives in full sun and in well-drained, enriched soil and requires water throughout the season. Divide plants every three years to maintain vigor. Related to the annual marjoram, *O. Majorana*.

♣ Ruta graveolens (Rue)
Shrub. Blue-green foliage on woody plant. Clusters

of tiny yellow blossoms in spring. To 36″. Thrives in full sun and in poor soil. Drought resistant. Plant in spring after all danger of frost. Cut back each spring to encourage bushiness and pinch plant throughout season to encourage branching habit. Foliage, sap, and oil is irritating to skin and can cause a rash.

♣ Salvia officinalis (Sage)
Perennial. Bright-green or deep-burgundy quilted foliage with lovely violet blossoms in tiered clusters in mid- to late spring. To 36″. Thrives in full sun and in ordinary soil. Drought resistant. Plant in spring after all danger of frost. Excellent for foliage color accents in borders. Select *S. officinalis* 'Purpurascens' for purplish tones and 'Tricolor' for variegated white, which, because it is tinged with purple, appears pink.

♣ Santolina Chamaecyparissus (Lavender cotton)
Perennial. Silver gray foliage, sporting miniature golden buttonlike blossoms in early summer. To 18″. Prefers full sun and enriched soil. Will also grow in partial shade. Drought resistant. Plant in spring after all danger of frost. Prune each spring to encourage vigorous growth during season. Do not cut to ground in fall as new foliage grows on old wood. Divide every three years to keep plant vigorous. In colder climates, mulch plants late in the fall and uncover them in early spring.

♣ Stachys byzantina (Lamb's ears)
Perennial. Low mat of woolly, silvery white foliage. To 6″. Flower stalks are unattractive. Prefers full sun and well-drained ordinary soil. Also thrives in partial shade. Drought resistant. Plant in spring after all danger of frost or fall. Divide every two years for more! Some gardeners remove the flower stalks, which is not a lot of work to maintain a beautiful plant that can be used either as a groundcover or an accent in beds.

♣ Tanasetum vulgare (Tansy)
Perennial. Bright-green, fernlike foliage, sporting clusters of brilliant gold buttonlike blossoms in late summer. 24–36″. Prefers full sun and ordinary soil. Drought resistant. Plant in spring after all danger of frost. Divide every other year and replant for continuing vigor.

Thymus (Thyme)

Perennial. Many varieties of low-growing, matlike plants in bright green and bluish gray, with silver, yellow, or white variegations, sporting tiny flowers in pink, purple, white, or rose, depending on variety. Prefers full sun but will thrive in partial shade and ordinary soil. Drought tolerant, but results are better with regular watering. Plant in spring after all danger of frost or transplant rooted cuttings throughout the season. Shear each fall to maintain vigor. Recommended varieties include:

Thymus X *citriodorus* (Lemon thyme): Distinct lemon scent with green foliage and rose-lavender blossoms. 'Aureus' has bright green leaves edged in cream; 'Argenteus' has gray-green leaves edged in white. 4–12″.

T. Herba-barona (Caraway-scented thyme): Narrow foliage with rose-pink blossoms. 2–5″.

T. praecox arcticus (Mother-of-thyme): Matlike dark green foliage with white or purple blossoms. To 4″.

T. pseudolanuginosus (Woolly thyme): Matlike gray woolly foliage with pink blossoms. ½″.

T. vulgaris 'Argenteus' (Silver thyme): silver white variegated foliage. 6–15″.

T. vulgaris (Garden thyme): spreading mounds with gray green leaves. 6–15″.

Groundcovers

Unless otherwise noted, all species included are hardy perennials and can be planted in spring or fall.

Achillea tomentosa (Woolly yarrow)

Yellow, tightly structured flower heads on fernlike foliage. 3″. Thrives in enriched, sandy soil, in full sun. Drought resistant once established. Deadhead spent blooms to encourage repeat bloom.

♣ Ajuga (Bugleweed)

Blue, purple, or white blossoms on vigorous, semi-evergreen plants with dark-green, burgundy, bronze purple, or variegated foliage, depending on variety. 4–10″. Thrives in ordinary soil, in full sun or partial shade. Drought resistant. If you wish a less vigorous variety to use in a garden scheme, select *A. genevensis* (Geneva bugle).

Alyssum saxatile, see *Aurinia saxatilis*

Arabis caucasica (Rock cress)

White or rose-pink clusters of blossoms over silver-green tufted foliage. 12″. Thrives in ordinary, gritty, well-drained sandy soil in full sun. Requires moisture, but is drought resistant once established. Plant in fall. One of the earliest blooming perennials, well-suited to a rock garden or border as well.

♣ Arctostaphylos Uva-ursi (Bearberry)

A ubiquitous low-growing North American native, with evergreen foliage that turns bronze in fall and sports brilliant red berries. Thrives in poor, sandy soil in hot sun. Drought resistant. Particularly attractive and maintenance free. Best groundcover for secondary dune areas.

♣ Arenaria verna 'Caespitosa' (Moss sandwort)

Spring-blooming, white, starlike blossoms on delicate, mosslike foliage. Thrives in full sun or partial shade in ordinary soil. Drought resistant. Ideal for tucking into wall cracks or between stepping stones.

♣ Armeria maritima (Thrift)

White or deep rose blossoms on semi-evergreen foliage. 4″. Thrives in ordinary, sandy soil, in full sun or partial shade. Drought resistant. One of the best groundcovers for seaside gardens. Very easy to propagate.

Aronia melanocarpa, see *Shrubs*

♣ Artemisia Schmidtiana (Silver mound)

Grown for its silver colored foliage. To 24″. Thrives in poor, sandy soil in full sun. Drought resistant (resents watering). Foliage can be dried and used in arrangements or for Christmas decorations. Excellent groundcover for secondary dune areas.

♣ Artemisia Stellerana (Beach wormwood)

Another silvery plant, with small clusters of yellow blossoms. To 24″. Native to the East Coast. Thrives in poor, sandy soil in full sun. Drought resistant (resents watering). Excellent groundcover for secondary dune areas.

♣ Aurinia saxatilis (Gold dust)

Brilliant sulphur-gold clusters of blossoms in spring, on silvery-gray foliage. 6″. Thrives in ordinary soil and prefers full sun. Drought resistant. Plant in early spring. Usually sold as *Alyssum saxatile*. 'Citrina' is a pale yellow version, more subtle than the brilliant yellow varieties.

Calluna vulgaris (Heather)

Tiny, white, pink, or red blossoms spikes in summer or fall on evergreen foliage. 18″. Thrives in poor soil, in full sun. In partial shade, bloom will be less profuse. Needs some moisture.

♣ *Cerastium tomentosum* (Snow-in-summer)

White blossoms in June on woolly gray foliage. 6–10″. Thrives in poor soil and in full sun, and has been known to prosper in pure sand. Drought resistant.

♣ *Ceratostigma plumbaginoides* (Blue plumbago)

Stunning deep blue blossoms in late August through late fall on glossy deep-green foliage that turns bronze in cold weather. 6–12″. Thrives in full sun or light shade, in ordinary soil. Drought resistant. Can become weedy if not contained.

Cornus canadensis (Bunchberry)

Yellow blossoms with white bracts in spring on medium-green foliage. 4″. Needs a moist, organic soil and partial shade. Edible berries persist through autumn. This North American woodland native is not hardy south of Zone 6.

Cotoneaster, see Shrubs

Erica carnea (Spring heath)

Spring-blooming cousin of heather, with red, pink, or white spikes of blossoms on evergreen foliage. 18″. Thrives in poor soil, in full sun. In partial shade, bloom will be less profuse. Needs some moisture.

♣ *Euonymus Fortunei* (Winter creeper)

Deep green evergreen foliage with pale red fruit in summer and fall. Thrives in full sun or partial shade and in poor soil. Drought resistant. Look for low-growing varieties, many of which have variegated foliage in white, pink, or yellow.

Gaultheria procumbens (Wintergreen)

Low creeping evergreen native with inconspicuous white flowers in spring followed by scarlet fruits in midsummer on shiny dark green leaves. 6″. Thrives in partial shade and in moist sandy soil. The aromatic leaves were once used to make oil of wintergreen and can be used to brew wintergreen tea. Not hardy south of Zone 7.

Hedera helix (English ivy)

Ivy, always grown for its handsome foliage, which ranges from deep green to yellow or white variegations depending on the variety chosen, can be trained either as a vine or a groundcover. Thrives in ordinary soil, in full sun or deep shade, and once established is drought resistant. Prune every fall to keep in bounds.

Holcus lanatus 'Variegatus', see Grasses

♣ *Hypericum calycinum* (Saint-John's-wort)

Big bright yellow blossoms in late summer on medium-green foliage. 6″. Thrives in full sun and in sandy soil. Drought resistant. Foliage turns purplish in fall. Hardy from Cape Cod south, but somewhat iffy in Maine.

English ivy

♣ *Iberis sempervirens* (Candytuft)

Clusters of white blossoms on lustrous, needlclike evergreen foliage. 6–24″. Thrives in full sun and in ordinary soil. Drought resistant. Many improved varieties now available. The dwarf *I. saxatilis* (rock candytuft) is particularly attractive.

♣ *Lamium maculatum* (Dead nettle)
Clusters of while blossoms on a plant grown mostly for its silvery-white and green variagated foliage. 12″. Thrives in light shade and in ordinary soil. Drought resistant. A Long Island favorite is *L. maculatum* 'White Nancy.'

♣ *Leiophyllum buxifolium* (Sand myrtle)
Native to southeastern coastal areas. Small, waxy white blossoms in May on evergreen foliage. Thrives in full sun and in ordinary soil. Drought resistant. Sand myrtle is not all that attractive a plant, but it will survive in secondary dune areas.

♣ *Liriope spicata* (Creeping lilyturf)
Lilac to white blossoms on spikes in mid- to late summer, on green grasslike foliage. 8–12″. Thrives in full sun or partial shade in ordinary soil. Drought resistant. To propagate, divide in spring and space plants 2–3″ apart.

Mitchella repens (Partridgeberry)
East coast woodland native. Small white or pink flowers in late spring followed by red berries, on a creeping groundcover with round, dark green, evergreen leaves. Thrives in partial shade in ordinary soil.

♣ *Opuntia humifusa* (Prickly pear)
Surprise! The only cactus plant hardy in northern climates. Large yellow or orange blossoms on thorny cactus foliage. 5–12″. Thrives in full sun and in sandy soil. Drought resistant. Weeding prickly pear can be agony, as the thorns are very sharp and it spreads rampantly. Frequently sold as *O. compressa.*

Pachysandra terminalis
White blossoms in spring on deep glossy green or variegated foliage. Prefers partial shade or deep shade and ordinary soil. Once established it is drought resistant, but prolonged drought will kill it. Propagates easily from cuttings or from unearthed, unwanted stock. Just wrap roots around finger and plant. When my late mother was young, she had a substantial planting of pachysandra on her property. Neighbors were envious, and so, every several days, she would pull some out, put it in a pail, and deliver it to various neighbors' doors. As a result she became known as "Notre Dame de Pachysandra."

Paxistima Canbyi (Cliff green)
Tiny white flowers on evergreen foliage. 1′. Thrives in partial shade and in acid soil and requires some moisture. Grow this East Coast native for its magnificent bronze autumn foliage.

Phlox divaricata (Wild blue phlox)
Lovely blue or lavender blossoms in spring on medium-green leaf clusters. Prefers partial shade and thrives in ordinary soil but needs moisture. Spreading stems put down roots.

Phlox stolonifera (Creeping phlox)
Purplish blossoms on mats of foliage in spring. 6–12″. Prefers shade and ordinary soil and is drought resistant once established. A native plant that adapts well to seaside environments.

Phlox subulata (Moss pink)
Small white, pink, or pale blue clusters of blossoms in mid-spring, on matlike, semi-evergreen foliage. 6″. Thrives in full sun or partial shade in ordinary soil. Drought resistant once established. A better choice than *P. stolonifera,* with many new varieties in clear colors available.

Polemonium caeruleum (Jacob's ladder)
Small, cup-shaped blue or white blossoms in mid to late spring on delicate medium-green mounds of foliage. To 15″. Thrives in either sun or shade, in average soil. Drought resistant once established. Plant in spring only. 'Blue Pearl' and 'Album' are recommended varieties.

Rosa Wichuraiana, see Roses

♣ *Sedum* (Stonecrop)
Scores of varieties with white, pink, yellow, gold, red, or blue blossoms on jade-green, yellow, purple, red, or gray succulent foliage. Prefers full sun and ordinary soil. Drought resistant. Plant at any time during the season. A few varieties are invasive. *S. spectabile* 'Autumn Joy,' the most spectacular cultivar, sports large mauve-pink flower heads that turn brilliant rust in fall on succulent, jade green foliage. To 36″. Research into available varieties is well worth the effort, for some are exquisite.

♣ *Sempervivum* (Hens-and-chickens)
The perfect companion for sedums has elegant

rosettes of succulent foliage in reds, greens, and blue-grays. Stalks of bizarre blossoms emerge in early summer. Prefers full sun and ordinary soil. Drought resistant. Research into available varieties is worth the effort.

Stachys byzantina, see Herbs

Thymus, see Herbs

Veronica (Speedwell)

There are many varieties of veronica, but only a few can be grown as groundcovers. Most offer purple, white-pink, or blue blossoms on pale-green or deep-green foliage. Prefers full sun and ordinary soil. Drought resistant once established. *V. Allioni* has spikes of purple blossoms over leathery deep green foliage. 4″. *V. filiformis*, the familiar lawn pest, with small pale blue blossoms on dense mats of medium green foliage, is very invasive. Taller growing varieties are not appropriate for use as groundcovers.

Sedum and American beach grass

♣ Vinca minor (Periwinkle, creeping myrtle)

This familiar groundcover has medium-blue or white blossoms on attractive glossy green foliage. 6″. A very versatile plant in terms of adapting to the environment, it thrives in full sun, partial shade, or deep shade, in ordinary soil. Drought resistant. Can be invasive if conditions are ideal.

Ferns

Ferns can be useful in the seaside garden, although they will not thrive in beach or dune environments. Use them in areas farther away from the sea, or where soil has been substantially improved. Most ferns require moisture during the summer drought period. The ferns listed below are deciduous, so you should remove spent foliage after a killing frost. All are hardy to Zone 5.

Adiantum pedatum (Maidenhair fern)

Native fern with lacy, soft green foliage. 18–24″. Prefers deep to light shade, rich moist well-drained soil, and moisture throughout the growing season. Plant in spring.

141

Variegated Bergenia and hosta, Japanese painted fern, and tall growing lady fern light up a shady corner

Athyrium Filix-femina (Lady fern)

Deep-cut, bright yellow-green foliage. 24–48″. Prefers partial shade, ordinary soil, and moisture throughout growing season. Plant in spring.

Athyrium Goeringianum 'Pictum' (Japanese painted fern)

Coarse gray-green and red foliage. 12″. Prefers partial shade, as sun leaches out color. Needs enriched soil with considerable amounts of organic matter worked in. Water regularly during growing season. Plant in spring.

Matteuccia Struthiopteris (Ostrich fern)

Yellow-green, feathery fronds. 3–6′. Prefers deep to light shade. Needs enriched soil with considerable amounts of organic matter worked in. Water regularly during growing season. Plant in spring.

Osmunda cinnamomea (Cinnamon fern)

Native fern with deep green, waxy textured fronds on cinnamon-colored stalks. 3–4′. Prefers deep to light shade. Needs enriched soil with considerable amounts of organic matter worked in. Water regularly during growing season. Plant in spring.

Osmunda regalis (Royal fern)

Native fern with deep, forest-green fronds. 4–6′. Prefers deep to light shade and slightly acidic soil, Water regularly during growing season. Plant in spring.

Grasses

Bloom times refer to peak time for plumy panicles or seed heads, not for blossoms, as grasses do not sport bloom. All cultivars included are hardy throughout the United States unless otherwise indicated.

♣ Ammophila breviligulata (American beach grass)

Open-spreading grass. Native grass with narrow, whiplike leaves. 12″. Your first line of defense against beach erosion. Prefers full sun and sandy soil. Drought resistant once established. This vigorous grower can be propagated easily by division of the rootstock. The first grass to plant to stabilize dunes or hold sandy soil.

Beach plum and American beach grass.

Cortaderia Selloana 'Pumila' (Compact pampas grass)

Ornamental grass. Silky panicles on tall bluish clumps. 4–6′. Thrives in full sun in ordinary soil. Provide moisture during extended summer drought until established. Not hardy north of Long Island. Plant in spring or fall. Cut foliage to ground before spring growth commences.

♣ Elymus arenarius (European dune grass)

Open-spreading grass. Green grass to 8″, sporting 10″ long spikes. Thrives in full sun, in sandy soil. Drought resistant once established. Provide moisture during extended summer drought. Plant in spring or fall. Can be established on dunes with American beach grass.

Festuca (Fescue grass)

Ornamental grass for massing. Grows in tufts to about 8″. Thrives in ordinary soil. Prefers dry conditions once established, but should be watered regularly during prolonged summer drought as roots like moisture. Plant in spring. Cut foliage to ground before spring growth commences. Many varieties are available, and some make good groundcovers.

♣ Holcus lanatus 'Variegatus' (Variegated velvet grass)

Ornamental grass for massing. Green and white variegated leaves. 8″. Tolerates sandy soil. Drought resistant once established. Cut foliage to the ground before spring growth commences. Can be grown as a groundcover.

Imperata cylindrica rubra (Japanese bloodgrass)
Ornamental open-spreading grass. Erect, pointed foliage with red tips. 12–24″. Plant in partial shade for most leaf color. Tolerates poor soil and dry spells but should be watered regularly during prolonged summer drought. Plant in spring. Cut foliage to ground before spring growth commences. Not hardy north of Long Island.

Miscanthus
Ornamental grass. Broad grassy foliage with silvery-tan plumes in midsummer. 4–7′. Prefers partial shade but tolerates full sun. Plant in ordinary soil. Tolerates dry spells but should be watered regularly during prolonged summer drought. Plant in spring or fall. Cut foliage to ground before spring growth commences. Useful seaside species include M. *saccariflorus* (silver banner grass), M. *sinensis* 'Gracillimus' (maiden grass), and M. *sinensis* 'Zebrinus' (zebra grass).

Panicum virgatum (Switch grass)
Ornamental grass. Finely cut green foliage. 4–7′. Delicate cloudlike blooms from midsummer to fall. Prefers full sun and ordinary soil. Water regularly as roots prefer moisture (species is native to Eastern salt marshes). Plant in spring or fall. Cut foliage to ground before spring growth commences. Bloom persists through winter and adds interesting touch to winter landscape. Attractive garden varieties with leaves that turn red in the fall ('Rehbraun,' 'Rotstrahlbusch,' 'Rubrum') are not as tall.

Pennisetum alopecuroides (Fountain grass)
Ornamental grass. Very fine arching foliage. 3–4′. Rose-tan foxtail-shaped bloom from midsummer through fall. Prefers full sun and sandy soil. Tolerates dry spells, but should be watered regularly during prolonged summer drought. Plant in spring. Cut foliage to ground before spring growth commences. Not hardy north of Long Island.

♣ *Phyllostachys* (Bamboo)
Running bamboo. Mature culms to 30′ (15′ in confined spaces) sporting fanlike foliage. Thrives in full sun or partial shade and in sandy soil. Tolerates dry spells when established, but should be watered regularly during prolonged summer drought (P. *nigra*—black bamboo—has greater drought tolerance). Most available varieties are hardy to Zone 7 and some to Zone 5.

Saturate transplanted bamboo daily for ten days. Older culms should be thinned out every autumn after five or six years. To curb spread of established groves, a barrier of sheet metal or concrete should be sunk 24–30″ into the ground. Bamboo is a good soil binder, is edible, and the culms are useful for constructing fences and trellises. People either love it or find it terrifying.

♣ *Uniola paniculata* (Sea oats)
Open-spreading grass. Native to southeast coastal United States. Grassy foliage from 2–5′. Thrives in full sun and sandy soil. Drought resistant. Plant in spring. Not hardy north of Long Island. Can be established on dunes with American beach grass.

Roses

The world of roses is too large to cover in a brief list, and I recommend that you familiarize yourself with the varieties of roses that thrive in your area. Roses can be used as shrubs, hedges, climbers, and groundcovers, but all need at least six to seven hours of full sun a day. Most require fortified soil and a reasonable amount of care, including watering, feeding, spraying, and pruning, in order to fulfill their potential. The three main classifications of roses are wild roses, old garden roses (often called "old fashioned roses"), and modern roses (hybrid tea roses), and each group includes shrub and climbing varieties. Among roses, the shrubs tend to be larger and more sprawling than the stiffer bushes, which are traditionally reserved for planting in beds. Here are some of the types you might encounter in plant catalogues, with some recommendations.

Old garden roses
These roses, such as Cabbage, Damask, Gallica, and Alba roses, the pride of nineteenth-century horticulture, are now enjoying a renewed popularity with gardeners. Not only are they intensely fragrant, but their bloom is profuse, most are disease resistant, and some even drought resistant, making them a good selection for a seaside garden. Unlike hybrids,

they offer one seasonal blooming in the spring. Many grow into large, somewhat unruly, plants and they need space to be displayed at their best advantage.

Modern roses

These large-flowered varieties, formerly called hybrid teas, are the best known of all roses. Most are compact bushes 3–5′ tall that produce single flowers on long stems. Some are fragrant, but many are not. These are the roses that, as a rule, take the most care to grow. So-called Grandiflora roses, which are produced by crossing large-flowered and cluster-flowered roses, are somewhat larger plants that produce up to a half dozen blooms on each stem. They are also more vigorous and most are fragrant. Cluster-flowered roses, formerly called Floribunda roses, are small 2–4′ bushes that are extremely vigorous, hardy, and disease resistant. They are usually covered with blossoms, which are smaller than large-flowered or Grandiflora roses. 'Betty Prior' is a pink cluster-flowered rose that has long been popular in America because it will grow dependably almost anywhere, even on the seashore. Polyantha roses are low-growing with small flowers in great abundance. Few Polyanthas are of interest today (they were popular in the 1920s), but one worth trying as a groundcover is 'The Fairy,' a virtually indestructable, disease-free plant with pink flowers and glossy green leaves. Finally, there are English roses, magnificent new hybrids that are the culmination of nearly forty years of research and rose breeding by David Austin of Great Britain. They are the result of crossing old garden roses with modern bush roses. For form and flower, delicacy of coloring, and rich fragrance, they can be compared with Damask, Gallica, and Alba roses, and they bloom repeatedly throughout the season. Because they are less demanding of ideal conditions than other modern roses, they are a good bet for a seaside garden.

Shrub roses

There are both modern and wild shrub roses. They grow 3–5′ depending on variety, with white, pink, red, yellow, or orange-toned blossoms. These are tough plants, and if they are happy, they become thick hedges with profuse bloom. Wild shrub roses are a good selection for difficult seaside areas, especially the *Rosa rugosa*. This marvelous plant first

Catnip under rugosa roses

Variegated porcelain vine and climbing hydrangea

flowers in late spring on 6′ canes with deep green leathery foliage, and then repeatedly throughout the summer. Brilliant red rose hips follow bloom, and the foliage turns bright orange in the fall. A very hardy species, it is especially good for seashore plantings because it can tolerate drought, poor soil, and salt spray, and can even be found on dunes facing the ocean. The species has a pink and a white form (*R. rugosa alba*). Also worth considering are the Hybrid Rugosa shrub roses, which are its descendants ('Frau Dagmar Hartopp' is much admired). Another wild shrub rose to consider is *R. Wichuraiana* (memorial rose), which bears small, white blossoms in late summer on glossy green, semi-evergreen foliage. The plants form mats that lie flat on the ground. Because it tolerates heat, drought, poor soil, and salt spray, it's an excellent groundcover for dune areas. Finally, *R. nitida*, a wild native to 2′ with small rose-colored blossoms and small hips after bloom, is a charming plant that is more manageable for the small garden than the *rugosas*. The lustrous, deep green foliage turns brilliant red in the fall. This is one of the few roses that will tolerate poor drainage.

Climbing and rambling roses

The world of climbing roses is a large one, and includes modern roses, old garden roses, and wild roses. If you have the space, include climbers in your planting scheme, as they offer extravagant bloom. The plants do not attach themselves to surfaces, but must be tied to trellises, fences, and other supports. Many grow to 10–20′. The very pale pink 'New Dawn' is a popular large-flowered climber that is very hardy and can also be grown as a large shrub. A wild rambler that is both famously hardy and profuse in its bloom is the pale yellow *R. banksiae lutea* (Lady Banks's Rose), spring flowering and fragrant. It needs full sun. Ramblers have long, wandlike shoots that bear clusters of small flowers, and are ideal for filling open spaces or growing over a pergola or other structure. Two old reliable white ramblers are 'Sander's White' and 'Seagull.'

Miniature Roses

These are lilliputian versions of the larger varieties growing to a mere one foot and sporting tiny blossoms. If space is a problem, and you want to grow roses, these are the best option.

Vines

Perennial vines are hardy to Zone 5, with many hardy to Zones 3 and 4. Annual vines will be killed by early frosts. Note that maximum growth height given is for optimal conditions; many vines will be substantially less vigorous in seaside conditions.

Ampelopsis brevipedunculata (Porcelain vine)
Perennial. Grown primarily for its appealing fruit, clusters of pea-shaped berries that turn from pale lilac to yellow and finally to blue in the fall. Bright green, textured foliage. Thrives in ordinary soil, in full sun or partial shade. Some drought tolerance, but water during dry spells. Plant outdoors in midspring or early fall. A vigorous grower suitable for secondary dune areas. *A. brevipedunculata* 'Elegant' has variegated leaves.

♣ *Campsis radicans* (Trumpet vine)
Perennial. Scarlet, orange, or yellow trumpetlike blossoms on vigorous vines with medium-green foliage. Grows to 50′. Thrives in ordinary soil in full sun or partial shade. Drought resistant. Plant outdoors in mid-spring or fall. Do not plant on or near the facade of a house or outbuilding, as vines grow through any openings. I have one in the wrong place on my property that I have been trying to kill for twenty years, and yet every year it sports new shoots and grows. Its hardiness is an asset near the sea, and it is ideal for secondary dune areas.

♣ *Celastrus* (Bittersweet)
Perennial. Grown for the orange and red berries that appear on the vines in fall. Thrives in ordinary soil in full sun or partial shade. Drought resistant. Plant outdoors anytime during the season. *C. scandens* is the native American bittersweet. The vines will choke any plant they climb on, including shrubs and trees, so be sure to keep them well-pruned or plant them where they cannot attach to other plantings. Good selection for secondary dune areas.

Clematis
Perennial. White, pink, red, blue, yellow, lavender, purple, and combinations thereof. Saucerlike blossoms 1–9″ in diameter, depending on variety, on vines sporting handsome medium-green, glossy

foliage. The flowers are followed by silvery seed pods. Thrives in moderately fertile, slightly alkaline soil, in full sun or partial shade (the base of the plant should be shaded to keep roots cool). Requires moisture during summer drought. Plant in early to late spring. When planting, dig a hole 2′ across by 2′ deep and fortify the soil with substantial amounts of peat moss or compost so that moisture will be retained around the roots of the plant. This is essential to vigorous, healthy growth. Virtually carefree once established.

Pruning clematis is a complicated business, since some varieties should be cut back to about 1′ in late winter and others should merely be pruned to remove dead vines or to shape or contain plant. It is best to check at point of purchase about pruning the particular variety that you have selected. The same holds true for the variety's growth habit, which may vary from 3′ to 30′. By the way, if you prune your clematis the wrong way, you won't kill it; at worst, you may deprive yourself of blooms for that season.

♣ *Clematis paniculata* (**Sweet autumn clematis**)
Perennial. Masses of fragrant, small white blossoms in late summer on vigorous, 20–30′ tangled vines with attractive, medium-green foliage. Thrives in ordinary soil, in full sun or partial shade. Drought resistant once established. Plant outdoors in mid-spring. A vigorous, yet easily controlled plant.

♣ *Hydrangea anomala* subsp. *petiolaris* (**Climbing hydrangea**)
Perennial. Large, flat, 6–8″ white or ivory blossom clusters and attractive deep-green foliage. To 75′. Thrives in enriched soil in partial shade. Requires moisture, but is drought resistant once established. Plant outdoors in mid-spring. Usually sold as *Hydrangea petiolaris*. Can be trained to grow up the trunks of tall trees or buildings.

Ipomoea (**Morning glory**)
Annual. Blossoms of sky blue, purple, pink, rose, red, white, or combinations thereof, on vigorous vines with large, heart-shaped, deep-green foliage. Thrives in ordinary soil, in full sun. Requires moisture. Plant outdoors, in situ, after all danger of frost, according to package directions. Soak seeds overnight in lukewarm water to hasten germination. The all-time favorite is the lovely *I. tricolor*

'Heavenly Blue,' which dresses up any garden from midsummer to killing frost.

♣ *Lathyrus japonicus/L. latifolius* (**Beach pea, perennial pea**)
Perennial. Purple to rose-colored pealike blossoms on short vines with medium-green foliage. Thrives in ordinary soil, in full sun or partial shade. Plant outdoors in mid-spring or fall. A vigorous plant suited for dune plantings. Annual *L. odoratus* (sweet pea) is also popular in seaside gardens.

♣ *Lonicera* (**Honeysuckle**)
Perennial. A very large genus of plants with many varieties available. All sport delicate, fragrant, spiderlike pink, red, yellow, or white blossoms on vigorous, compact vines with medium-green foliage. Most offer berry displays in the fall. Most thrive in ordinary soil, in full sun. Drought resistant. Plant outdoors, from early spring to fall. For secondary dune areas, where vigorous, invasive growth is desired, select *L. tatarica*. Do not use this plant in sheltered seaside areas as it will take over the entire garden in no time flat.

♣ *Parthenocissus tricuspidata* (**Boston ivy**)
Perennial. Ivy-shaped leaves of deep lustrous green that turn brilliant red in the fall. To 35′. The insignificant blue berries that appear in the fall are relished by birds. Thrives in ordinary soil in full sun or partial shade. Drought resistant. Plant outdoors in mid-spring or fall. An excellent plant for stone walls or facades, but will cover wooden stockade fences as well.

Phaseolus coccineus (**Scarlet runner bean**)
Annual. Brilliant scarlet, pealike blossoms on 15′ vines sporting medium-green foliage. Thrives in ordinary soil, in full sun or partial shade. Requires moisture. Plant outdoors, in situ, after all danger of frost. Rapid and strong summer growth. Train on trellises, posts, or fences.

♣ *Polygonum Aubertii* (**Silverlace**)
Perennial. Panicles of white flowers in late summer, on medium-green foliage. To 20′. Thrives in sandy soil, in full sun. Drought resistant. Twining vine grows rapidly but will not harm shingles or wood walls.

Roses, climbing, see Roses.

♣ *Smilax glauca* (Catbrier)
Perennial. Semi-evergreen native plant with medium-green leaves bearing blue-black berries in the fall. Vines occasionally have thorns. Thrives in ordinary soil in all light conditions. Drought resistant. Plant anytime from early spring to late fall. Suitable for secondary dune plantings. Too rampant for sheltered gardens.

♣ *Tropaeolum* (Nasturtium)
Annual. Yellow, orange, gold, and red funnel-shaped blossoms on 3–5' vines bearing pretty pea-green leaves. Thrives in ordinary soil in full sun (if soil is too rich, foliage will be lush but flowers will be few). Requires moisture during drought. Plant seeds outdoors after all danger of frost according to package directions. Deadhead for continuous bloom. The pungent foliage is edible and can be used in salads.

♣ *Vitis Labrusca* (Fox grape)
Perennial. An ancestor of American cultivated grapes, with grapelike leaves and small purple, amber, or brown-red grapes in fall. Thrives in ordinary soil, in full sun or partial shade. Drought resistant. Plant in spring or fall. Attracts Japanese beetles, so if you grow roses in your garden avoid this plant. Suitable for secondary dune areas. Too rangy for sheltered gardens.

♣ *Wisteria floribunda*/*Wisteria sinensis* (Japanese/Chinese wisteria)
Perennial. White, purple, lavender, or pink, highly fragrant, blossom clusters, 9–20" long on vigorous vines , with medium-green loosely structured foliage. To 50'. Thrives in ordinary soil, in full sun. Drought resistant once established. Plant in early spring. Avoid fertilizing plant as this will diminish bloom substantially. Wisteria often needs heavy pruning, particularly if planted on a trellis or pergola adjoining a house or near trees. It has been known to destroy a house if allowed to grow unchecked, but its vigor is an asset by the sea.

Shrubs

All shrubs included in this list are hardy to Zone 5, with many hardy to Zones 2 and 3.

♣ *Aronia arbutifolia* 'Brilliantissima' (Chokeberry)
Deciduous native shrub. White five-petaled blossoms in spring followed by bright red berries, on medium-green foliage which turns bright red in autumn. 3–8', but can be controlled by pruning. Prefers moist conditions, but will thrive in seaside gardens. If possible, water regularly during summer drought.

♣ *Aronia melanocarpa* (Black chokeberry)
Deciduous native shrub. White blossoms in spring and black berries in fall on medium-green foliage. 18–36". Use as a groundcover.

♣ *Baccharis halimifolia* (Groundsel, sea myrtle)
Deciduous native shrub or small tree. White, thistlelike blossoms in late summer on coarse, yellow-green foliage. 4–10', but can be controlled by pruning. Groundsel is highly tolerant of salt spray and can be planted very near the shoreline in sandy soil. Drought resistant.

♣ *Berberis Thunbergii* (Japanese barberry)
Deciduous shrub. Red berries in fall and foliage of red, yellow, purple, dark green, or with variegations, depending on variety. 2–5'. Thrives in sandy soil. Drought resistant. A compact, thorny shrub often used for hedges because it takes pruning well. The thorns tend to collect debris, which can be difficult to remove

♣ *Buddleia Davidii* (Butterfly bush, summer lilac)
Deciduous shrub. Showy lilaclike spikes of white, yellow, deep blue, pink, red, or purple clusters of blossoms on medium-green foliage. 6–15', but can be controlled by pruning. Drought resistant. Foliage dies down to the ground in the winter, growing again to mature height in spring. Cut back to 4–6" in late fall or early spring before new growth commences.

♣ *Buxus* (Box)
The traditional evergreen shrub for hedges, tightly branched, with small lustrous leaves. 3–6', depending on variety, of which there are many in cultivation. Thrives in sun or partial shade and in ordinary soil. Drought tolerant once established. Not hardy north of Zone 6 and not used more widely because of its susceptibility to extreme cold. Dwarf forms are ideal for edging beds.

Caryopteris X clandonensis (Bluebeard)
Deciduous shrub. Spikes of blue or purplish blue blossoms in late summer and fall on silvery green foliage. 3–4'. Cut back to 6" in late winter or early spring. If location is ideal, plant will self-sow. You can avoid seedlings by cutting all flowering stems after bloom, but you may find the plant so attractive and useful that you will want lots of them to transplant elsewhere in the garden. Hardy to Zone 5.

Ceanothus ovatus (Wild lilac)
Deciduous native shrub. Small clusters of white blossoms on medium-green foliage. To 3'. This, and C. americanus, which is too rangy in habit for garden use in my opinion, is the only variety of Ceanothus appropriate for temperate regions. The popular C. X Delilianus grows only in subtropical climates.

Chamaecyparis (False cypress)
Coniferous shrub. Globular, pyramidal, and spreading forms in silver, blue, green, or gold foliage, depending on variety. Recommended dwarf varieties include:
C. obtusa 'Aurea Nana' (Dwarf gold Hinoki cypress): Heavy gold foliage.
C. obtusa 'Kosteri Nana': Lacy foliage, broad growth habit.
C. obtusa 'Tortulosa Nana' (Dwarf twisted branch cypress): Branches are twisted; compact irregular pyramidal form.
C. obtusa 'Gracilis Nana': Deep-green foliage, upright growth habit.
C. pisifera 'Argentea Nana' (Dwarf silver cypress): Soft plumed silvery blue foliage; dense globular growth habit. 'Argentea Variegata Nana' has variegated foliage.
C. pisifera 'Aurea Pendula' (Dwarf gold thread cypress): Bright golden pendulous filaments; dense low-growing shrub. Does not burn in sun.
C. pisifera 'Minima' (Dwarf threadleaf cypress): Green foliage; compact growth habit.
C. pisifera 'Sulphuria Nana' (Dwarf sulpher cypress): Bright sulpher-colored foliage; broad growth habit.
C. pisifera filifera 'Aurea Variegata Nana' (Dwarf gold variegated cypress): Gold variegated foliage.

♣ **Clethra alnifolia (Sweet pepperbush, summersweet)**
Deciduous native shrub. Spikes of white or pink

flowers in late summer followed by black seeds that look like peppercorns, on medium-green foliage. 4–6'. Thrives in wet or dry sandy soil and in sun or partial shade. Tolerant of salt spray.

Comptonia peregrina (Sweet fern)
Deciduous native shrub. Fernlike shrub with aromatic leaves. Requires moisture in normal soil. A refreshing tea can be made from the leaves. Adapts to wetland conditions.

Cornus sericea (Red osier dogwood)
Deciduous native shrub. Small white blossoms in late spring and white berries in summer, on medium-green foliage. To 7'. The red bark is particularly lovely in the snow. C. sericea 'Flaviramea' (golden-twig dogwood) sports yellow stems.

♣ **Cotoneaster**
Broad-leaved evergreen shrub. A wide range of cultivars either upright or creeping, most with white or pink blossoms in spring and red berries in fall, on lustrous, deep-green foliage. 2–20', depending on variety. Drought resistant once established. Cotoneaster is especially useful to cover a sunny bank or to control erosion. Varieties that are tough and fast growing and are particularly suited to the seaside garden include:
C. Dammeri (Bearberry cotoneaster): Low-growing (18") and useful as a groundcover, although technically a shrub.
C. divaricatus (Spreading cotoneaster): A carefree shrub that sports brilliant yellow and red long-lasting foliage in the fall, to 6'.
C. horizontalis (Rock cotoneaster): Another lower growing variety (24–36") that makes a beautiful fall display.

♣ **Cytisus scoparius (Scotch broom)**
Deciduous or semi-evergreen shrub. Yellow, crimson, apricot, lilac, and tricolor, pealike blossoms on upright shrub with needlelike foliage. To 6'. Thrives in full sun and in sandy soil. Drought resistant. Tolerant of salt spray. In the landscape, the small, inconspicuous foliage offers a nice contrast to the more lush foliage of other shrubs.

Forsythia
Deciduous shrub. Yellow or cream-colored blossoms in early spring, on upright or weeping shrub with

bright green foliage. 6–8′. Avoid weeping versions as they require annual pruning to keep them under control once established. Upright varieties such as *F. X intermedia* 'Linwood Gold' are recommended. Prune after flowering rather than in fall or early spring for most profuse display each season.

♣ *Gaylussacia baccata* (Huckleberry)
Deciduous native shrub. Reddish flowers followed by dark blue edible berries. Small green leaves turn red in fall. To 36′. Thrives in wet or dry sandy soil. Drought resistant.

♣ *Genista* (Broom)
Deciduous or semi-evergreen shrub. A group of useful plants for the seaside environment, similar to *Cytisus*. Select from the following: *G. tinctoria* (dyer's greenweed), now naturalized in the eastern part of the United States, with yellow pealike blossoms in early June that can be used to make yellow dye, to 36″; *G. sagittalis* (arrow broom), an excellent ground cover (to 20″) in sandy soil and hot sun, with yellow pealike flowers in late spring. Drought resistant.

Hebe
Broad-leaved evergreen shrub. White or pink blossoms on leathery foliage. Like pachysandra, *Hebe* can be easily propagated from cuttings. Two varieties are appropriate for seaside gardens: *H. X Andersonii*, a white, late-summer blooming species, to 4′. 'Variegata,' with leaves edged in cream, is widely available; *H. decumbens* (ground hebe), with small gray leaves edged in red and small spikes of white blossoms in spring.

♣ *Hibiscus syriacus* (Rose-of-Sharon, althaea)
Deciduous shrub or small tree. An old fashioned favorite, cultivated in North America for over two hundred years. White, white and burgundy, or rose blossoms, resembling the southern hibiscus, on medium green foliage. To 15′. Recent hybrids, such as 'Diane', a pure white, are stunning. Nearly indestructible.

♣ *Hippophae rhamnoides* (Sea buckthorn)
Deciduous shrub. Willowlike gray-green foliage with silvery underside. Small, white blossoms are inconspicuous, but fall berries are bright orange and profuse. To 30′. Thrives in full sun and sandy soil.

Drought resistant. Male and female plants are necessary for fruiting. As the berries are very acidic, birds are not attracted to them and they persist throughout the fall and into winter.

Hydrangea macrophylla (French hydrangea)
Deciduous shrub. The classic summer seashore plant. Large blue, white, or pink pompon-shaped blossoms in mid- to late summer, on handsome deep-green foliage. 3–6′. Tolerates shade. Roots prefer moist conditions, so be sure to provide sufficient water during summer drought. Plant will tell you if it needs watering by wilting visibly. If you want blue bloom, try scratching one tablespoon of an acid fertilizer such as Miracid into the ground around the plant when shoots first emerge in spring. For pink bloom, substitute one tablespoon of garden lime.

♣ *Juniperus* (Juniper)
Coniferous shrub. Creeping, low and spreading, vase-shaped and columnar, with varying shades of green, blue, or gold foliage. The toughest of the junipers is *J. conferta* (shore juniper), a low spreading shrub (12–24″ high to 8′ in width) that will often grow directly on ocean dunes. Other recommended varieties include:
J. chinensis 'Japonica' (Japanese juniper): Semi-upright in habit; deeply textured foliage in slate to green shades.
J. chinensis 'Blue Vase' (Blue vase juniper): Vase-shaped growth habit, to 5′.
J. chinensis 'Old Gold' (Old gold juniper): Golden yellow in color.
J. chinensis 'Pfitzerana Aurea' (Gold tip juniper): Bright golden color in spring and summer.
J. chinensis 'Torulosa' (Hollywood juniper): Dense shrub with twisted branches, to 6′.
J. chinensis var. *procumbens* 'Nana' (Dwarf Japanese juniper, Pronina juniper): Short stiff branches forming a carpet up to 6′ across, mounding to 10″ in the center.
J. horizontalis 'Bar Harbor' (Bar Harbor juniper): Creeping form; steel blue foliage with a fernlike appearance.
J. horizontalis 'Blue Chip' (Blue chip juniper): Silvery blue foliage; spreading, low mounding habit.
J. horizontalis 'Glauca' (Blue creeping juniper): creeping form, blue foliage.
J. horizontalis 'Plumosa' (Andorra juniper): Low

spreading habit; summer foliage silvery green turning purple after frost.
J. rigida 'Pendula' (Weeping needle juniper): Narrow, tall, and pendant in habit.

♣ *Kolkwitzia amabilis* (Beautybush)
Deciduous shrub. My own feeling is that beautybush is overused in North America, but this 10′, medium-green foliaged shrub thrives in dry sandy soil and can be used as a windbreak. Drought resistant. Most specimens sport washed-out pink blossoms, but look for deeper pink blooming plants at local nurseries, often called 'Rosea'. Seed clusters follow the blossoms and the brown bark falls from stems in long strips. Autumn foliage is red.

♣ *Ligustrum* (Privet)
Deciduous or semi-evergreen shrub. Privet bears white flower clusters in the spring, but is of course grown primarily for its glossy foliage. To 15′. The ubiquitous hedging plant used for windbreaks and privacy screening. Drought resistant. High pruning the trunk results in an interesting treelike form. There are numerous varieties to choose from, especially of *L. ovalifolium* (California privet) and *L. vulgare* (common privet).

♣ *Myrica pensylvanica* (Bayberry)
Semi-evergreen native shrub. Silvery-gray berries in autumn on glossy foliage. To 9′, although usually 4–5′. Berries are used to make bayberry oil and bayberry candles. Thrives in sand and withstands salt spray. Drought resistant. Can be grown very close to the ocean.

Pieris japonica (Andromeda)
Broad-leaved evergreen shrub. Small clusters of white blossoms in spring on lustrous 3½″-long leaves. 6′. Andromeda is one of the earliest of the broad-leafed evergreens to bloom and therefore useful in combination with early spring blooming bulbs such as daffodils and hyacinths. Thrives in partial shade and moist soil.

Pinus, see Trees

Potentilla fruticosa (Bush cinquefoil)
Deciduous native shrub. Small yellow or white blossoms throughout summer and into fall on foliage that resembles strawberry leaves. To 4′. Will not bloom unless grown in full sun. Survives in poor, dry soil with little moisture, but, of course, will grow better in enriched soil and with regular watering. There are many named varieties available. 'Beesii,' 'Katherine Dykes,' and 'Vilmoriniana' sport silver foliage.

♣ *Prunus maritima* (Beach plum)
Deciduous native shrub. A dense, compact shrub, to 6′. White flowers in the spring become small blue or red plums that can be made into delicious jelly or jam. Leaves turn red in the fall. Thrives in full sun. Tolerates sandy soil, shade, wind, and salt spray. Drought resistant. Hybridizers have been busy creating varieties that produce larger fruits with red color, such as 'Eastham,' 'Hancock,' and 'Premier.'

Prunus pumila (Sand cherry)
Deciduous shrub. White flowers and purple-black fruit on purple foliage. To 8′, but can be contained by pruning. Tolerates sandy soil.

Rosa, see Roses

Spiraea varieties (Bridal wreath)
Deciduous shrub. Graceful arching branches completely covered with white, pink, or red blossoms in late spring, on medium-green foliage. To 6′, depending on variety. Needs sun and is not drought tolerant. Prune in fall every few years to maintain vigor: remove branches at soil level, not by cutting them half-way down. Fountain-shaped *S. X Vanhouttei* is the most commonly planted variety.

Symphoricarpos orbiculatus (Coralberry)
Deciduous shrub. A densely branched plant grown for its colorful purple-red berries in the fall. The spring yellow blossoms are inconspicuous. 7′. Roots help retain bank or dune soil. *S. orbiculatus* 'Leucocarpus' sports white berries.

Syringa (Lilac)
Deciduous shrub or small tree. Pink, white, lilac, blue, or deep-purple clusters of florets in late spring on medium-green foliage. Thrives in full sun. *Syringa vulgaris* (common lilac) is too tall (it grows to 20′) for borders, but can be used for screens or planted in a grove in the distance. Lilacs that grow to a more manageable height and thrive in a seaside environment include *S. X persica* (Persian lilac),

with deep purple blooms (6') and *S. oblata dilatata* (Korean early lilac), with pink blooms (5–6'). Deadhead flowers for more profuse bloom following year.

♣ *Tamarix* (Tamarisk, salt cedar)
Deciduous shrub or small tree. Fluffy pink blossoms in the spring on feathery foliage. To 15'. Prune after bloom. Tolerates poor soil, wind, and salt spray. Drought resistant.

♣ *Taxus* (Yew)
Coniferous shrub. Medium to deep green needles on columnar, moundlike, and globular plants. Drought resistant. The following varieties are particularly useful in the seaside garden: *T. cuspidata* 'Densiformis' (spreading Japanese yew), a mound-shaped shrub, spreading to 6', with medium-green needles, that can be sheared to make hedges; *T. Fairview* (Fairview yew), globular and compact in growth habit; and *Taxus* 'Aurea Nana' (golden dwarf yew), a dwarf with bright yellow-green foliage.

Thuja occidentalis (American arborvitae)
Coniferous native shrub. Pyramidal, conical, globular, and columnar forms with gold and light to dark-green foliage. American arborvitae, which grows to 60', can be dwarfed by vigorous pruning and tolerates salt spray and sandy soil. Two valuable varieties are 'Hetz's Midget' (dwarf globe arborvitae), a slow growing, globular shrub with medium-green foliage and 'Woodwardii' (Woodward globe arborvitae), a bushy shrub that can even be used in window boxes.

♣ *Vaccinium corymbosum* (Highbush blueberry)
Deciduous native shrub. Another tried and true classic for the seaside garden. Inconspicuous white flowers followed by blueberries that ripen in early summer on handsome deep green foliage that turns brilliant red in the fall. 6–12'. Drought resistant and adapts to wetland conditions.

♣ *Viburnum*
Deciduous shrub. Viburnums prefer sun and tolerate salt spray. Recommended varieties include:
V. Carlesii: Waxy fragrant blossoms, tinged pink in early spring, on gray-green foliage that turns bronze-red in fall, to 6"; shapely growth habit.
V. dentatum (Arrowwood): A native that adapts to wetland conditions, with attractive clusters of white blossoms in spring, followed by blue berries, on deep green foliage which turns bright red in autumn, 8–14'.
V. Opulus (European cranberry) or *V. trilobum* (American cranberry): Large, flat clusters of white blossoms in spring followed by bright red fruit, on handsome deep green foliage that turns bright crimson in fall, to 12'. Select varieties of either listed as 'Compactum,' 6', or 'Nanum,' 2–3', if space is at a premium. These species are almost identical, but some horticulturists hold that *V. trilobum* has better autumn color, and it is a native that has adapted equally well to wetland and shoreline conditions. The fruit is edible but not to everyone's taste.
V. prunifolium (Black haw): An old-fashioned favorite for seaside plantings, with flat, white clusters of spring blossoms and blue-black fruit in late summer and fall, on dark green foliage that turns maroon then deep red in fall, growing to 15' but very accepting of pruning as either a shrub or small tree. Plants are dense enough to form hedges, with fruit that has been used in preserves since the Colonial era.

Weigela
Deciduous shrub. Scarlet, trumpet-shaped blossoms in late spring-early summer, on medium-green foliage. 5–6'. Prefers partial shade where summers are hot. *Weigela* requires little care, but after a few years old flowering wood should be pruned at soil level after the shrub blooms.

Trees

Trees on this list have been divided between evergreens, particularly conifers, and deciduous trees, which lose their leaves in the fall. Generally speaking, the mature height of trees depends entirely on growing conditions. Specimens grown near the ocean rarely reach their full height and are subject to a phenomenon called wind pruning

EVERGREEN TREES

Abies concolor (White Colorado fir)
Pyramid form. Blue-green, 2″ needles. To 120′. Prefers full sun and ordinary soil and is drought resistant once established. Of all the evergreens, this is perhaps the most heat resistant. Among the best selections are 'Violacea,' with bluish-white needles, and 'Conica,' which is a slow-growing dwarf variety.

♣ *Cedrus atlantica* 'Glauca' (Blue Atlas cedar)
Pyramid form. Tight whorls of short, silver-green needles. To 120′. Attractive cones persist through winter. Prefers full sun and ordinary soil. Drought resistant once established. Atlas cedar is one of the most handsome evergreens for seaside plantings.

♣ *C. Deodara* (Deodar cedar)
Pyramid form. Elegant tree with weeping branches and somewhat longer needles than Atlas cedar. To 150′. 'Pendula' has branches that often touch the ground; 'Glauca' has blue-green or silver-gray needles. Prefers full sun and ordinary soil. Drought resistant once established.

♣ *Chamaecyparis* (False cypress)
Conical or columnar forms. A very large group of evergreen trees with very small, scalelike leaves, in various shades of green, blue-green, and silver, many with variegated coloring of yellow, white, or silver. Most thrive in full sun and tolerate drought conditions and sandy soil. Consult locally for recommended cultivars.

Cryptomeria japonica (Japanese cedar)
Conical form. Elegant evergreen with small, short needles. 6–150′, depending on variety. Bark shreds, creating trunk interest. Consult locally for recommended cultivars.

♣ *Ilex* (Holly)
A large group of useful trees and shrubs suitable for seaside environments. Hollies generally need sun to fruit out successfully, as well as a well-drained light soil. They are dioecious, which means that there needs to be a male within about one-half mile of a female if you want fruiting trees. Both sexes bear flowers, but only the female bears berries. Recommended varieties include:

I. cornuta (Chinese holly): Large, dark, shiny green leaves and red fruit. Compact form. 'Dwarf Burford' can be sheared into a dense, formal hedge. Drought tolerant, but not reliable north of Zone 7. Female plants set fruit without a male plant.

I. crenata (Japanese holly): Fine, glossy leaves and small black fruit. Various forms, most adaptable to shearing for hedges. Needs protection in Zone 6.

I. glabra (Inkberry): Inconspicuous black berries in late summer and fall on deep-green shiny oval leaves. Male and female plants are necessary for fruiting. Tolerates salt spray but not very dry soil. Responds well to pruning.

I. opaca (American holly): The hardiest holly. Dark green leaves and small red or orange fruit. Conical or open form, to 50′, but much shorter on the shore. Native to seashore environments Long Island and south. Can be used for tall hedges. Many varieties available.

I. pedunculosa (Longstalk holly): Glossy oval leaves and red fruit on 1½″ stalks. Similar in habit to American holly.

I. verticillata (Winterberry): Native deciduous shrub with many available garden varieties sporting different leaves and berries ranging from red to orange to yellow, 4–15′. Plant red-fruiting cultivars to attract birds. Winterberry grows best in full sun in very wet soil, but drought tolerant varieties are available.

I. X altaclerensis (Highclere holly): Large glossy leaves, often spineless, and red fruit. Small tree or large shrub. Somewhat tolerant of salt spray, but not reliable north of Zone 7.

I. X Meserveae (Blue holly): Spiny blue-green leaves and red fruit. Rounded, compact form, 5–8′. Can be used for low, informal hedges. Not reliable north of Zone 6.

♣ *Juniperus virginiana* (Eastern red cedar)
Native, tough, and planted everywhere. Conical or columnar form. Slow growing tree with small, scalelike leaves and blue cones that resemble berries.

100', but rarely exceeds 30' near the shore. Thrives in full sun in ordinary to poor soil. Drought resistant once established. Can be used as a screen or hedge. Many varieties available.

♣ *Picea* (Spruce)

A large group of trees with short blue or green needles in mounded, conical, pendulous, and columnar forms. Thrives in full sun or partial shade and in ordinary soil. Drought resistant once established. Dwarf or slow-growing varieties suitable for seashore gardens include:

Picea glauca var. *albertiana* (Alberta spruce): Conical dwarf with medium-green needles.

Picea mariana 'Nana' (Dwarf black spruce): Mound-shaped with short, light grey-green needles.

Picea pungens 'Glauca' (Dwarf blue spruce): Conical dwarf with blue needles.

Picea pungens 'Globosa' (Dwarf globe blue spruce): Globe-shaped tree with silvery blue needles.

♣ *Pinus* (Pine)

A large group of trees with long needles in shades of green and blue-green in mounded, columnar, pendulous, and conical shapes. Thrives in full sun or partial shade in ordinary soil and resists drought once established. Recommended dwarf varieties include:

Pinus Mugo (Mugo pine): Low growing (and slow growing) moundlike pine with long, bright green needles. Very hardy.

P. pumila (Dwarf Siberian stone pine): Spreading habit with light blue-green to blue needles.

P. Strobus 'Nana' (Dwarf white pine): Bushy habit with feathery blue-green needles.

P. Strobus 'Ontario' (Dwarf Ontario white pine): Spreading habit with feathery blue-green needles.

P. sylvestris 'Watereri' (Dwarf Scotch pine): Compact slow growing form of Scotch pine, conical when young becoming rounded with age. Recommended taller varieties include:

P. rigida (Pitch pine): A scrubby native with dark green needles that thrives in very difficult rocky or sandy soil, especially at the seashore. To 75'.

P. sylvestris (Scotch pine): Compact, bushy tree adapting well to seaside conditions. Very hardy.

P. Thunbergiana (Japanese black pine): An irregular, conical pine with bright green needles that thrives in a seashore environment. However, be advised! Despite the fact that this tree is almost universally recommended for seaside use, especially for windbreaks, a disease is killing them everywhere. Seek the advice of a knowledgeable gardener or your local Cooperative Extension agent before planting.

DECIDUOUS TREES

Acer griseum (Paperbark maple)

Dark-green trifoliate leaves cast light shade and develop good fall color. Bark is an especially attractive cinnamon brown and strips from trunk naturally throughout growing season. Roundish shape to 25'. Prefers sun or partial shade and ordinary soil and is moderately drought resistant once established. All maples have surface roots that absorb most of the moisture from the surrounding soil. Underplant only with shade loving, drought resistant groundcovers or install pebbles or wood chips to retain moisture.

A. platanoides (Norway maple)

An excellent shade tree, roundish in shape and densely branched, with dark-green, leathery leaves. To 80'. Prefers sun or partial shade and ordinary soil and is drought resistant once established. Autumn foliage is brilliant yellow or orange-red. Norway maple has brittle branches that tend to split and break during heavy windstorms, and some people feel it is already too intensively used. Consult locally for recommended cultivars.

♣ *A. pseudoplatanus* (Sycamore maple)

Especially suited to a seaside environment. If you have space for one large tree, select this one. Five-lobed leaves in various colors, depending on variety. To 90'. Prefers sun or partial shade and ordinary soil and is drought resistant once established. There is no colorful autumn foliage display. Consult locally for recommended cultivars.

A. rubrum (Red maple)

This native maple is not the familiar Japanese maple. It derives its name from the fact that its spring blossoms are bright red. Dark-green leaves and excellent fall color. Fast growing to 40', it splits easily during windstorms. Prefers full sun or partial shade. Consult locally for recommended cultivars. Adapts to wetland conditions.

Amelanchier canadensis (**Shadbush, shadblow, serviceberry, Juneberry**)
Small native tree sporting single white flowers in early spring, followed by silver-gray foliage that turns yellow and red in fall. 6–20′, but can be controlled by pruning. Thrives in ordinary soil. Colorful, reddish-purple fall berries are relished by the birds. The more vigorous *A. arborea* is similar, and has larger flowers. Adapts to wetland conditions.

Betula pendula (**European white birch**)
Pyramidal weeping tree with white bark and small, glossy dark-green leaves. To 60′. Prefers full sun and normal soil and is drought resistant once established. Tree has brittle branches, making it susceptible to damage in heavy winds, is subject to bronze birch borer infestation, and is short-lived, but its white bark is irresistible. The native white birch, *B. populifolia*, is a smaller tree that often has multiple trunks. Consult locally for recommended cultivars.

♣ *Catalpa speciosa* (**Northern catalpa**)
Distinguished by its large handsome leaves and clusters of white blossoms in summer, which are followed by long pods. Fast grower to 90′. Prefers full sun and ordinary soil. Drought resistant. A popular tree for difficult areas because it is vigorous in hot, dry environments.

♣ *Celtis occidentalis* (**Hackberry**)
Native shade tree with glossy dark-green leaves and dark-purple fruits that attract birds. Good yellow fall color. 30–60′. Prefers full sun and ordinary soil and is drought resistant. Hackberry is a good choice for difficult areas because it tolerates hot, dry environments, but it is subject to a number of diseases, including leaf disfiguration.

Cercis canadensis (**Redbud**)
Early spring-flowering native, offering a profusion of small, purple-pink blossoms that are followed by dried pods later. Heart-shaped leaves turn a brilliant yellow in the fall. 25′. Prefers full sun and ordinary soil and is drought resistant once established. *C. canadensis alba* sports white blossoms.

Crataegus (**Hawthorn**)
This small tree bears either white or pinkish-red blossoms in spring and red fruit in summer. Leaves

are a glossy dark green and autumn foliage is brilliant red. Prefers full sun and ordinary soil and is drought resistant once established. *C. crus-galli* (cockspur) and *C. Phaenopyrum* (Washington hawthorn), both natives, are the two best cultivars for all environments, both growing to 25′. Because their branches are thick with razor sharp thorns, hawthorns are not a good tree to plant where children play. An unarmed variety of cockspur is available.

♣ *Elaeagnus angustifolia* (**Russian olive**)
Spreading shrublike tree distinguished by its elegant, silvery foliage. Yellowish flowers in early spring are followed by silver berries in fall. 12′. Thrives in full sun and in sandy soil, and is tolerant of saltspray. Drought resistant. Grows fast and likes an occasional pruning. Birds are attracted by berries. *Elaeagnus umbellata* (autumn olive) is similar.

Fraxinus (**Ash**)
A fast growing native shade tree, with handsome compound foliage. 50–80′. Prefers full sun and ordinary soil and is drought resistant once established. This vigorous tree is an excellent selection for seaside gardens. Select either *F. americana* (white ash), spectacular in yellow and purple in the fall, or the tougher *F. pennsylvanica* (green ash), with darker leaves and a more modest fall display.

♣ *Gleditsia triacanthos* var. *inermis* (**Honey locust**)
Delicate bright-green foliage and fragrant pendulous clusters of white blossoms in late spring. 30–70′. Autumn foliage is yellow. Good drought and salt tolerance. If you like the tree but not the seedpods that litter the ground in late summer, there are seedless varieties available.

Malus (**Flowering crab apple**)
Beautiful small tree, bearing white, pink, or deep red blossoms in spring. Many varieties offer edible small, red crab apples in summer and fall (technically, crab apples are apples under 2″ in diameter). To 25′. Prefers full sun and moist soil, but is drought resistant once established. Dwarf and semi-dwarf varieties are available for use on patios and for small gardens. Standard sized trees can be used as specimen trees, in borders, as backdrops. It

154

is a good idea to check at a reliable local nursery for the names of varieties recommended for your particular area.

♣ *Nyssa sylvatica* (Pepperidge, sour gum, black gum, beetlebung, or black tupelo)

An East Coast native whose many common names testify to its wide appeal. Handsome leathery, dark-green leaves turn brilliant orange to scarlet in fall. 30–50'. Thrives in full sun or partial shade, and in ordinary to moist soil. Drought resistant and also adapts to wetland conditions. Purchase only small specimens, since taproot damage can kill tree.

Platanus X *acerifolia* (London plane)

This hybrid of native and European cultivars is an excellent tree for difficult areas where there is lots of space for it to spread. Large, coarse maplelike leaves and exceptional bark. 75–100'. Prefers full sun and ordinary soil, and is drought resistant once established. Familiar street tree.

Prunus cerasifera (Flowering plum)

Small flowering tree with white flowers in early spring followed by edible plumlike fruit and glossy leaves. To 25' Prefers full sun and ordinary soil, and is drought resistant once established. Look for varieties with purple leaves, like 'Nigra,' 'Rosea,' or 'Thundercloud.'

♣ *Prunus serotina* (Black cherry)

A native tree, sporting white flowers in spring followed by small red fruits that turn black when mature. Elegant, lustrous foliage. To 60'. Easily grown, prefers full sun, ordinary soil and is drought resistant once established. Birds love the fruit, which can be used for sauces and desserts.

Quercus alba (White oak)

The sturdy, familiar native tree. Dark green lobed leaves turn purplish red in autumn. To 90'. Slow growing. Prefers full sun and ordinary soil. Drought resistant once established.

Q. palustris (Pin oak)

Dense, native of swampy woodlands. Graceful, drooping branches with glossy jagged leaves that turn brilliant red in fall. To 75'. Thrives in full sun and ordinary soil. Drought resistant once estab-lished. Note that oaks are usually substantially dwarfed when grown in a seaside environment.

Robinia pseudoacacia (Black locust)

Native with light-green oval leaves bearing pendulous clusters of fragrant white blossoms in late spring. To 75'. Prefers full sun and ordinary soil. Drought resistant once established. Consult with local nurseries regarding new disease resistant varieties.

♣ *Salix* (Willow)

A large group of deciduous trees and shrubs, some of which grow well in seaside environments. S. *Matsudana* 'Tortuosa' (corkscrew willow, dragon-claw willow) with twisted shoots and leaves, makes an interesting specimen tree. To 20'. It is tolerant of sandy soil and some salt spray, and is drought resistant.

♣ *Sassafras albidum* (Sassafras)

Interesting native of coastal forests. Bright-green lobed and mitten-shaped leaves leaves turn bright orange and red in the autumn. 30–60'. Prefers full sun and ordinary soil and tolerates seaside conditions, including some salt spray. Drought resistant. Dried root bark is the source of the familiar flavoring agent.

Syringa reticulata (Japanese tree lilac)

Small tree valued for its cream colored blossoms clusters in early summer. To 30'. Thrives in full sun and ordinary soil. Drought resistant once established. Some people feel that the blossoms have a bad smell, so plant away from house or outdoor living areas.

Tilia cordata (Littleleaf linden)

Small, dark-green, heart-shaped leaves give tree an elegant look. To 90'. Thrives in full sun and ordinary soil. Drought resistant once established. Littleleaf linden takes pruning well and can be shaped or even trimmed as a hedge. Check locally for new varieties that are appropriate for your area.

SOURCES

Books on Seaside Gardening

Foley, Daniel J. *Gardening by the Sea from Coast to Coast.* Radnor, Pennsylvania: Chilton Book Company, 1965. An excellent book with a thorough plant list and useful information.

Menninger, Edwin A. *Seaside Plants of the World: A Guide to Planning, Planting and Maintaining Salt-Resistant Gardens.* New York: Hearthside Press, 1964. Primarily aimed at the gardener in Southern California and Florida, this book is difficult to use but worthwhile finding for its list of 2,000 plants for seaside use, rated in terms of three "belts."

Schmidt, R. Marilyn. *Gardening on the Eastern Seashore.* New Jersey: Barnegat Light Press, 1993. Contains a useful plant list for East Coast gardeners. Available from the publisher: Barnegat Light Press, Box 305, Barnegat Light, NJ 08006.

Schmidt, R. Marilyn. *Seashore Plants by Mail.* Pine Barrens Press, 1993. This indispensible book lists 228 suppliers of seaside plants with addresses. Available from the publisher: Pine Barrens Press, Box 305, Barnegat Light, NJ 08006.

Sources for Plants

There are hundreds of excellent sources for seaside plants. The following list provides a useful starting point for the beginning gardener. Experienced gardeners will want Schmidt's *Seashore Plants by Mail,* listed above.

Bulbs

Van Bourgundien Bros., Box A, 245 Farmingdale Road, Rt. 109, Babylon, NY 11702. Phone: (800) 622-9997. The largest selection of bulbs available in the United States and the prices are very reasonable. Catalogue: free.

Perennial plants and shrubs

Bluestone Perennials, 7211 Middle Ridge Road, Madison, OH 44057. Phone: (800) 852-5243. One of the best sources for perennial plants at very reasonable prices. They have recently added shrubs to their offerings. Catalogue: free.

Wayside Gardens, Hodges, South Carolina 29695-0001. Phone: (800) 845-1124. A stunning collection of perennials, bulbs, roses, shrubs, and trees is offered. The free catalogue is extremely useful.

White Flower Farm, Litchfield, CT 06759-0050. Phone (203) 496-9600. A stunning collection of perennials, bulbs, roses, shrubs, and trees is offered. Catalogue: free.

Annual and perennial seeds

Park Seed Co., Cokesbury Road, Greenwood, SC 29647-0001. Phone: (800) 845-3369. An extensive variety of annual and perennial seeds is available here. Catalogue: free.

Thompson & Morgan, Box 1308, Jackson, NJ 08527. Phone: (800) 274-7333. This house offers the most extensive list of perennial and annual seeds in the country, many of which are unavailable anywhere but here. The free catalogue is extremely useful.

W. Atlee Burpee Co., 300 Park Avenue, Warminster, PA 18974. Phone: (215) 674-4900. This is another house that offers a great variety of annual and perennial seeds. Catalogue: free.

Roses

Jackson & Perkins Co., Box 1028, Medford, OR 97501. Phone: (800) 292-GROW. America's largest purveyor of roses. Catalogue: free.

Roses of Yesterday and Today, 802 Brown's Valley Road, Watsonville, CA 95076. Phone: (408) 724-3537. This house offers a comprehensive selection of old garden roses and some difficult-to-find modern roses. Catalogue: $3.00.

Royall River Roses, 70 New Gloucester Road, North Yarmouth, ME 04097. Phone: (207) 829-5830. Hardy roses grown in Maine, including a good selection of hybrid rugosa roses. Catalogue: free.

Grasses

Kurt Bluemel, Inc. 2740 Green Lane, Baldwin, MD 21013. Phone: (800) 498-1560. A broad selection of ornamental grasses, as well as bamboo and ferns. Catalogue: $3.00.

Water gardens

Lilypons Water Gardens, 6800 Lilypons Road, P.O. Box 10, Buckeystown, MD 21717-0010. Phone: (800) 999-5459. This firm provides everything you need to build a lily pond. Catalogue: $5.00.

ACKNOWLEDGMENTS

We wish to thank so many people for their enthusiasm, encouragement, and kind cooperation while we were working on this book. In Maine, special thanks are accorded Gene Skewis Moll and her husband Ed for their kindness, Katie Dennis for introducing us to so many gardeners in Northeast Harbor and Bar Harbor, Mrs. Thomas Hall, Jane Robinson, George and Linda Smith, and the many gardeners who permitted us to enter and photograph their extraordinary gardens.

On the east end of Long Island, designer Elizabeth Lear deserves special mention for her kind enthusiasm and for introducing us to so many designers, architects, and homeowners in the area. Their efforts are well represented in this book. Michael Graham of Deerfield, Frankenbach Nursery of Water Mill, Ellen Kosciusko, Seton Shanley, Robert Dash, Emerick Bronson, Kate Tyree, Charles and Helga Michel, Harriet and Walter Weyer, Dr. Rutledge W. Howard of Boerne, Texas, Douglas E. Ward of Normandy Beach, New Jersey, Betsy Trundle of Virginia Beach, Virginia, and Tim Cottrell also deserve mention for their kind assistance.

Special thanks are due to our editor Eric Himmel and his wife Caroline for inviting us to stay with them at their summer house on Fire Island and for introducing us to numerous gardeners in the area. Our thanks also to our literary agent, Rosalind Cole.

Finally, a special thanks to Tom Langhauser, whose keen eye and pre-dawn enthusiasm has enhanced the photographs.

INDEX OF PLANT NAMES

159